MW00768863

HAUNTED ENGLAND

Royal Spirits, Castle Ghosts, Phantom Coaches, & Wailing Ghouls

Also by Terence Whitaker

Books
Lancashire's Ghosts and Legends
Yorkshire's Ghosts and Legends
Dr Ruxton of Lancaster

Play
He'll Have to go, Mrs Lovejoy

HAUNTED ENGLAND

Royal Spirits, Castle Ghosts, Phantom Coaches, & Wailing Ghouls

TERENCE WHITAKER

DORSET PRESS

New York

This edition published by Dorset Press
a division of Marboro Books Corporation,
by arrangement with Contemporary Books, Inc.
1990 Dorset Press

ISBN 0-88029-471-X

Printed in the United States of America

M 9 8 7 6 5 4 3 2 1

First published in Great Britain 1987 by Robert Hale Limited.
Originally titled *Ghosts of Old England*.

For Marjorie and Julia
with love

Contents

All houses in which men have lived and died
   Are haunted houses; through their open doors
The harmless phantoms on their errands glide
      With feet that make no sound upon the floors.

                                Longfellow

Introduction

For over 2,000 years the British Isles have been known as 'The Islands of Ghosts' and for the early civilizations of the Mediterranean, 'going west' literally described the journey of the soul or the spirit after death. Britain, it was considered, was a Heaven, where the souls of the dead resided, whilst enjoying eternal feasting, gallant victories and idyllic love affairs.

Samuel Johnson, when asked for his views on the subject of ghosts, considered it to be, 'One of the most important that can come before human understanding. A subject which, after five thousand years, is yet undecided.' I don't expect through this book to determine the matter one way or another, but it does seem to me that either a large number of people have been victims of some kind of delusion – or ghosts really do exist.

It has been estimated that one person in ten will see a ghost at some time during their life, yet in twentieth-century Britain, the existence of ghosts is still either dismissed as rubbish or accepted supinely without question. Perhaps this is where the whole charm of the subject lies, the fact that no one can prove or disprove it. What is irrefutable, is that thousands of people say they have seen what they consider to be a ghost. And who are we to disagree? If a person says they have seen a ghost, there is no way of disproving it; they know what they have seen.

But whether the reader believes in ghosts or not, you have to agree we all enjoy a good ghost story. We all enjoy being frightened – always providing of course, we are in warm, convivial surroundings and in the company of others.

Sir Winston Churchill once wrote, 'A nation which forgets its past, has no future.' If that is the case, then the future of

Britain is assured, for there appears to be more interest in the history, legends and ghost-lore of the country today, than at any other time.

Perhaps this is a good point to insert a word of caution. In this book I have tried to provide a guide to a wide variety of haunted sites from the thousands I have collected over a period of nearly thirty years. Many of these locations are open to the public, but the reader should remember that a number of them are also private properties and I would ask you to respect this privacy.

So many people have been responsible for helping me write this book, it would be impossible to acknowledge them all by name. To the many newspaper and magazine editors; the radio and television presenters and the countless librarians who have gone to a great deal of trouble on my behalf and to the many individual contributors, I offer my sincere and humble thanks.

My thanks also to my wife Marjorie for her helpful suggestions and to my daughter Julia. They have both displayed much patience and understanding. To them and to all those who have contributed in any way, this book is dedicated.

Terence Whitaker

HAUNTED ENGLAND

Royal Spirits, Castle Ghosts, Phantom Coaches, & Wailing Ghouls

1. Haunted Castles

It's a poor castle that doesn't boast a ghost or two, and perhaps one of the most famous castles in the world is the Tower of London, whose ancient battlements, along with the colourful Beefeaters and legendary ravens, attract millions of tourists every year from all around the world. Strolling amongst the picturesque courtyards and buildings, they listen enthralled as guides bring to life the spectacular and violent events that shaped Britain's past. The Tower of London was once the most blood-drenched spot in the whole of England – and for nearly 800 years it has had ghosts to prove it.

One of the first ghosts ever recorded here was that of St Thomas Becket, who was seen in 1241, seventy-one years after his murder in Canterbury Cathedral. Becket, who was a Londoner, had in fact been Constable of the Tower before he became Archbishop of Canterbury in 1162. When his ghost returned to the Tower, it was seen by a priest who said he thought the Archbishop was objecting to some alterations and extension work which were being carried out. This work was thought to be upsetting people living close to the Tower walls, and it is recorded that the spirit was 'seen to strike the walls with a cross, whereupon they fell as if hit by an earthquake'.

Other ghosts have far more personal reasons for haunting the Tower. Perhaps the most frequently seen is that of Queen Anne Boleyn, the second of Henry VIII's wives. Over the years she has been spotted by several sentries, and one even had to face a court-martial because of her ghost.

The poor man was found unconscious outside the King's House on a winter's morning in 1864 and was accused of falling asleep whilst on duty. He told the hearing that, whilst he was on guard, a strange white figure had emerged out of the early morning mist. It wore a curious bonnet which appeared to be empty. When he challenged the figure three times and it continued to walk towards him, he ran the body through which his bayonet. As he did so, a flash of fire ran up his rifle barrel and he passed out. Other soldiers and an officer told the court-martial that they too had seen the apparition from a window of the Bloody Tower. After the court heard that the apparition had been seen just below the room where Anne Boleyn had spent the last night before her execution on 19 May 1536, the unfortunate sentry was cleared.

Anne Boleyn had a horror of dying at the hands of a bungling executioner, so her husband agreed to import an expert from France, allowing him to use a French sword for the beheading. However, once she was dead, all niceties ceased and her headless body was bundled into an old arrow chest and buried in almost indecent haste in the Tower chapel of St Peter ad Vincular.

Since then sentries have often seen her phantom figure pacing up and down outside the tiny church. One night a guard noticed an eerie light coming from one of the chapel windows. He climbed a ladder to peer inside and was astounded to see a ghostly procession of knights and ladies in Tudor dress file slowly up the aisle, led by a woman who resembled Anne. When she reached the altar, they all vanished, leaving the chapel in darkness again.

At about 2 a.m. one morning in February 1915, a sergeant and his watch saw a woman in a brown dress. She walked quickly towards the Thames, which runs past one side of the Tower, and disappeared into a stone wall. The last time Anne Boleyn's ghost was seen here was, to my knowledge at least, in February 1933. A sentry reported seeing her headless body floating towards him, close to the Bloody Tower. Because this spot is known to be one of the worst affected in the whole of the Tower, he was merely reprimanded for leaving his post.

Three other sixteenth-century ladies who lost their heads here are also known to haunt the Tower, Catherine Howard, the fifth of Henry VIII's six wives, was beheaded here in 1542, and she has been seen walking the walls at night.

Margaret, Countess of Salisbury, re-enacts the horrors of her execution in 1541, every anniversary. Perhaps she has just cause, for her death was admittedly one of the most horrific of the beheading ceremonies ever witnessed here. After being led screaming and struggling to the block, she escaped from her guards and ran around demented, whilst the formidable masked figure of the axeman chased her until she tripped and fell. The guards dragged her writhing body to the blood-stained block, as the axeman aimed his first blow. It missed. The second and third attempts also missed their mark, and the Countess must by then have been completely insane. She screamed incessantly and struggled to free herself from the men holding her down. The executioner, no doubt himself upset by the disturbance, made another attempt, only to tear open half his victim's neck. Her screams now turned to blood-filled gurgles and moans. It took five blows of the axe before the object was achieved and her head rolled to the ground. Is there any wonder then that she is still heard screaming in abject terror, near the site of the scaffold round about the time of the anniversary of her execution?

One of the more recent recorded sightings of a ghost at the Tower was in August 1970, when a young woman from Grays in Essex was in one of the rooms of the Bloody Tower. The apparition was that of a long-haired young woman, dressed in a long black velvet dress, with a white cap and with a long golden medallion hanging from her neck. The figure was standing by one of the open windows and, when the visitor walked towards her, vanished, leaving the visitor experiencing difficulty in breathing.

The witness was not in any way afraid, just puzzled as to who the apparition could have been. A very good case was put forward in an article in a London newspaper that this was probably the ghost of Lady Jane Grey, who reigned as queen for only nine days in 1553.

Two sentries recognized her when they saw the small figure of a woman running along the battlements of the inner wall, close to the Salt Tower, just after three o'clock on the morning of 12 February 1954. This happened to be the morning of the 400th anniversary of her execution on Tower Green, less than 200 yards away. On 12 February 1957, exactly three years later, two Welsh Guards sentries reported seeing a 'white shapeless form' on the Salt Tower, where Lady Jane Grey was imprisoned before her execution, at the age of seventeen.

Not all the ghosts in the Tower of London are those of women. Phantom men and children also roam the ancient walls.

In 1890 a sentry described an encounter so vivid he nearly died of fright. He reported that he was on duty in the Beauchamp Tower when he heard his name being called. He turned and saw, floating in mid-air, a red, bloated face, with a loose, dribbling mouth and heavy-lidded pale eyes. Recognizing the face from portraits in the Tower, he realized he was looking into the eyes of King Henry VIII, 'with all the devil showing in him'. During the First World War another sentry reported seeing a ghostly procession pass him near Spur Tower. A party of men were carrying a stretcher bearing the headless corpse of a man, his head tucked beside his arm. This was a regular practice in the old days when bodies were returned to the Tower for burial, following execution on Tower Hill.

The ghost of the Duke of Northumberland used to be seen so often walking between the Martin and Constable Towers that sentries nicknamed the pathway between the towers 'Northumberland's Walk'.

Sir Walter Raleigh was the favourite of Queen Elizabeth I, but he fell foul of her successor King James I and was executed in 1618. His ghost was reported many years ago, walking near the Bloody Tower, as were the ghosts of two young children, seen walking hand in hand. They are thought to be the shades of King Edward V and Prince Richard, the brothers allegedly murdered on the orders of their uncle in 1483, so that he could claim the throne of England – as King Richard III.

A ghostly monk has been witnessed in St Thomas's Tower. In 1952 the Keeper of the Jewel House awoke one morning to see a monk in a brown habit, walk through a closed door into his bedroom. Several Yeoman Warders (Beefeaters) have found themselves bundled out of bed by an invisible, mischievous spirit which haunts a bedroom in the Well Tower. In 1972 a photographer had set up his camera atop a ladder in the Beauchamp Tower, in the room where Lord Lovat, the last Tower prisoner to lose his head, was held. The photographer claimed he was roughly pushed as he reached the top of his ladder and was sent tumbling to the hard stone floor.

But perhaps the most unusual spectre reported by some of the military personnel is that of a bear, thought to be the sole survivor of the days when the Tower was used as a menagerie or perhaps for the occasional bear-baiting session. One day in October 1817 a sentry outside Martin Tower watched vapour pour through a narrow gap between the closed door and the sill. Horrified, he watched as the vapour took on the shape of a giant bear. The guard lunged at it with his bayonet, but the cold steel passed through the figure and stuck in the wooden door. The man collapsed from shock and never recovered, for within a few days he was dead.

The only current ghost at the Tower of London still appears to be that of little Lady Jane Grey, who, though one of the youngest, died with the full dignity of a Queen.

Tradition tells of many ghosts which are said to indicate the presence of buried treasure, or to be the guardians of it. Amongst these stories, that of the White Lady of Blenkinsopp Castle remains one of the most fascinating blends of truth and legend.

Blenkinsopp Castle stands on the borders of Cumbria and Northumberland, about eighteen miles from Carlisle. It was built over 600 years ago and, although the passage of time has taken its toll of the once magnificent building, the story of the restless, plaintive phantom said to haunt it has persisted strongly for several centuries.

According to tradition, the handsome Sir Bryan de Blenkinsopp was gallant and brave in battle, enjoying a very favourable reputation. However, like most men he had a weakness, and his was an inordinate love of wealth, a vice he cherished in secret until he rashly disclosed himself at the marriage of a brother knight to a lady of high rank and fortune. When, as the various toasts were made, the guests came to drink the health of Blenkinsopp and his future, he replied that he would never marry – not unless the lady concerned was able to bring him a chest of gold, heavy enough to defeat the efforts of his strongest men to carry it. This outburst was greeted with an astonished silence. Ashamed of having betrayed his thoughts, Blenkinsopp left the table and ran out of the castle.

It seemed that such a bride was not to be found and at length he quit his castle, the pleasures of the table with its gay company and the joys of the chase, and left the country. But he returned a few years later, bringing with him not only a foreign-born wife but also her dowry, a box of gold that took twelve of his strongest men to carry into the castle. There was a great feasting and rejoicing for the lord's return, and the fame of his new wealth spread far and wide.

But Blenkinsopp felt no deep love for his wife. Quarrels were a daily feature, and in her despair – hoping perhaps, that it might bring about a reconciliation – she, with the aid of her followers who had accompanied her to England, hid the chest of gold in some part of the castle during her husband's absence, refusing to give it up to him on his return. Furious, Blenkinsopp stormed out of the castle, never to return. After waiting for more than a year, the distressed wife, about whom very little was known outside the castle, took her attendants and left the neighbourhood in search of him. Neither she nor her husband was ever seen again. Their fates remain a complete mystery to this day.

There are those who argue that eventually the wife did come back and, filled with remorse at her conduct towards her husband, could not rest in her grave and wandered back to the castle to mourn over the chest of gold, the cause of their misery. This she was destined to do until someone with sufficient courage followed her and removed the treasure, so giving her spirit rest.

Over the centuries, there have been many recorded sightings of the ghost of a white lady, usually walking the castle grounds. In the eighteenth century a labourer on the estate and his family went to live in two of the more habitable rooms of the now run-down castle. The parents slept in one room, their children in the other. One night husband and wife were awakened by loud screams from the children's room and, rushing in, found one of the children sitting up in bed, terrified. 'The White Lady! The White Lady!' he screamed. The parents examined the room and found nothing, so, thinking the child had suffered a nightmare, they tried to re-assure him.

'She's gone,' replied the boy, 'and she looked so angry at me because I would not go with her. She was a fine lady – and she sat at my bedside, wringing her hands and crying sore. Then she kissed me and asked me to go with her and she would make me rich, as she had buried a large box of gold, many hundreds of years since, down in the vault and she would give it to me, because she could not rest as long as it was there. I told her I was scared and she said she would carry me, and lifting me up, I cried out. This frightened her away!'

Persuading themselves that the child had been dreaming, the parents managed to calm him and get him to sleep; but the following three nights they were roused in the same manner, the child repeating the same story. They had to take him from the room to sleep elsewhere, and only then were they no longer troubled by the ghost, although the boy would never afterwards enter any part of the old castle alone, even in daylight.

Up until about 1820, some poor families continued to live in a few of the better rooms in the castle, which was crumbling around them. Then all was left to ruin.

A number of years later, the occupier of a neighbouring farm ordered that the vaults underneath the old castle keep be cleared out, so that he could winter his cattle there. When the rubbish was removed, a small door, level with the bottom of the keep, was discovered. The entrance to a damp passage was cleared out, and it suddenly struck them that they had discovered the entrance to the White Lady's vault. Only one man was found who was brave enough – or stupid enough – to volunteer to enter the passage, which was quite narrow and hardly high enough for a man to stand upright in,

He walked forward for a few yards, descended a flight of steps and carried on again until he reached a doorway, whose door had long since crumbled away. Here the passage took a sudden turn, and he saw in front of him a steep flight of stone stairs. However, at this juncture, accumulated rubbish and foul air compelled him to give up. His candle died out and he had to grope his way back to the entrance.

The man tried a second time, but again his light was extinguished by the lack of air and, as the farmer had so little curiosity about the passage, he ordered that it be blocked up.

In 1875 the crumbling skeleton of the castle passed from the

Blenkinsopp family to Edward Joicey, who made a great effort to restore it. In five years the castle was almost completely re-built, only some of the walls and parts of the outer shell being retained. During this restoration work, the entrance to the secret passage was re-discovered. This passage was believed to be at least 1½ miles long, linking the castle with the stronghold at Thirlwall. Somewhere along it, the hidden treasure chest is thought to lie. But to date no more attempts have been made to explore it.

The castle remained the property of the Joicey family until 1951, when it was acquired by a new owner who announced he would attempt to trace the treasure, but so far as I can discover this never came about. In 1954 fire severely damaged the castle, leaving it a charred and roofless shell once more, with the exception of the west wing, which was bought and restored the following year, only to become a poultry farm and caravan site.

So, does the box of gold lie somewhere under the ruins of Blenkinsopp Castle? Would the White Lady, if she could, indicate its present location? Or has she gone to eternal rest and abandoned her earthly treasure forever? Certainly she has not been seen for well over ten years now.

Her Majesty the Queen freely admits she could quite happily live without the loyal subjects who regularly make their presence felt at Windsor Castle, and she likes to be kept informed whenever a ghostly intruder is encountered on her property.

Windsor Castle was built by William the Conqueror; many British sovereigns are buried there, and it is haunted by four of them: King Henry VIII, Queen Elizabeth I, King Charles I and King George III. The castle is also haunted by the ghost of a young guardsman who killed himself there in 1927.

The guardsman's ghost mainly haunts the old Deanery in the castle grounds and is mostly heard or seen at night, walking quickly past a bedroom until it reaches the bathroom. Often the noisy ghost appears to take four steps down, before resuming his hurried pace. This can possibly be explained by the fact that the floor in this part of the old house has been raised from its earlier level and, in the process, the steps have been eliminated. The ghostly guardsman has often been spotted by soldiers on sentry duty, and many who have spotted him in the Long Walk believe at first that he has come to relieve them.

In 1977 two soldiers claimed to have seen the bulky ghost of King Henry VIII walking along the castle battlements. They followed the figure and watched as it vanished into a wall. Later, inspection of plans of the ancient castle revealed that a door, long since bricked up, once existed at the precise point where the ghost disappeared. More recently, a young guardsman on duty at the castle collapsed after he claimed he had seen the King's ghost in the cloisters. The cloisters are, in fact, the favourite 'haunt' of Henry VIII, and ghostly groans and the sound of the old King dragging his ulcerated leg have been heard quite often in these passages.

In the Royal Library HRH Princess Margaret saw the figure of Queen Elizabeth I, the last Tudor monarch, who has wandered the twelfth-century castle since her death in 1603. It is said that Princess Margaret followed the figure into the room, but when she reached the door, the figure had vanished. Other witnesses to the ghost of Good Queen Bess include the Empress Frederick of Germany and a Lieutenant Glynn of the Grenadier Guards, who heard the tap, tap of high heels sounding on bare boards when he was in the Library. The sounds came nearer, and presently the stately figure of Elizabeth I drifted into view, passing so close to him that he could have reached out and touched her. She entered an inner room – from which there was no other exit – and although Lieutenant Glynn followed her immediately, he found no sign of the figure which he had witnessed walk through the deserted room.

Another ghost who seems to be quite at home in the Royal Library is that of King George III, who, prior to his death on 29 January 1820, had been confined to Windsor Castle during the last years of his lunacy. His ghost has been seen and heard in various rooms, often muttering one of his most-used phrases, 'What, what?'

The sad ghost of King Charles I, who lost his head in 1649 after the Civil War, has been reported seen here on many occasions too, standing beside a table in the Library. The

Canon's House, in the castle precincts, is also reported to be haunted by him, after a ghostly figure was recognized by its uncanny likeness to the famous van Dyck portrait.

A Coldstream Guardsman found unconcious in the Great Park in 1976 had experienced a different kind of ghost. He told those who found him that he had seen the ghost of Herne the Hunter, a man clad in deerskins and a helmet with antlers jutting from the forehead. King Henry VIII claimed to have witnessed this ghost himself, and over the last 250 years hundreds of people have said they have seen the same apparition, silently speeding through the castle grounds with his ghostly pack of hounds. When, in 1863, the tree from which Herne the Hunter allegedly hanged himself was cut down, Queen Victoria reserved the logs for her own fire, 'to kill the ghost'. Even so, this has not prevented the ghost of Richard II's forester from putting in an appearance from time to time.

Lancaster Castle, John of Gaunt's grim fortress standing alongside the River Lune, has seen more people sentenced to death than anywhere else in Great Britain. Over the centuries they were persecuted for their religious beliefs, for political crimes and, in a number of sensational trials in the seventeenth century, for allegedly practising witchcraft.

Many prisoners were brutally tortured behind the seven-foot-thick walls of Hadrian's Tower, where today are to be found many of the relics from this forbidding past. One can still see the branding iron that burnt the letter 'M' – for 'malefactor' – on a victim's hand; a scold's bridle, an iron mask with sharp, spiky points in it, used as a punishment for women who had been found guilty of spreading malicious gossip; thumb screws and other grim instruments of torture, and the deep, forbidding dungeons.

Some people still swear that part of the Tower wall drips with the blood of the wretched prisoners. A 'red, sticky substance' has been seen running between the crevices of the big wall blocks, and the moans and shrieks of the tortured victims have often been heard. Is it more than just a coincidence that one old reference book relates that, 'Blood oozed from every nook and cranny in Lancaster Castle'.

*

The castle at Hastings in Sussex is said to have been the scene of the first tournament in England, held in honour of a daughter of William the Conqueror. After the castle had ceased to be a stronghold in the twelfth century, it was used as a religious house, and today there are frequent reports of ghostly organ music being heard here.

A ghostly figure, believed to be St Thomas Becket, has been seen quite often on warm autumn evenings, within the castle precincts. There are also tales of the sounds of rattling chains and the groans of starving prisoners, echoing some tragic event many centuries ago. People say that on certain sunny, misty mornings a huge mirage of Hastings Castle can be seen on the horizon far out to sea, and strangely the castle appears once again in all its former glory, with flags and pennants flying from the turrets.

Who is the silent, shadowy figure said to haunt the ruins of Scarborough Castle, high above the seaside resort on Yorkshire's east coast? Most people seem to agree that this is the ghost of a Gascon immigrant by the name of Piers Gaveston, late Earl of Cornwall and one-time friend of King Edward II.

History tells us that it was here that Gaveston surrendered the castle to the barons some 600 years ago, on condition that his life be spared to stand trial. Gaveston had become increasingly unpopular with both peasant and noble alike, but when the Earl of Warwick laid siege to Scarborough Castle, he resisted valiantly for quite a time, before hunger and thirst finally forced the garrison to surrender.

Warwick promised Gaveston and his men safe conduct but, once the gates were opened, he treacherously broke his word and had Gaveston beheaded outside the castle walls. Now Gaveston's spirit, unable to rest because of the treachery of his enemy, prowls the castle ruins. A fearsome, headless apparition, he rushes towards those who are unlucky, or brave, enough to walk amongst the ruins after dark, and tries to chase them over the edge of the battlements.

The village of Berry Pomeroy, just a few miles from Totnes in Devon, was named after a Norman family responsible for building the attractive castle on the peak of a wood-covered cliff.

Here, from the Norman Conquest of 1066 until 1548, lived the de la Pomerai family. In about 1550 Edward Seymour, Duke of Somerset and brother of Jane Seymour, King Henry VIII's third wife, constructed a large mansion within the castle walls, whilst acting as Regent for young King Edward VI. The Seymours remained at Berry Pomeroy until late in the seventeenth century, when it was evacuated due to damage caused during the Civil War. However, the present owner, the second most senior Duke in the country, preceded only by the Duke of Norfolk, still prides himself in taking care of the castle, despite the fact that it suffered further damage from a disastrous fire in 1708.

Reports of hauntings at Berry Pomeroy Castle can be traced back many hundreds of years, but they became widely known only during the latter part of the last century, when an eminent physician, Sir Walter Farquhar, referred to it in his memoirs. Sir Walter recounted how he was called one day to attend the wife of the steward of the castle, who was very seriously ill. Whilst waiting to see the patient, he was shown into a lofty, oak-panelled room, which had a flight of stairs in one corner, leading to a room above. As he was looking round the room, the door opened and a beautifully dressed lady entered, wringing her hands and obviously in great distress. Taking no notice of the doctor, the woman walked across the room, mounted the stairs and then paused and looked directly at Sir Walter, who was able to see, before she disappeared, that she was a very young woman of remarkable beauty.

A few minutes later the doctor was ushered into the patient's bedroom and, seeing she was so ill, decided he would have to come again the following morning. To his surprise, when he called again the next day his patient was much better. Discussing the marked improvement with the patient's husband, Sir Walter then remarked on the beautiful lady he had seen on his visit the day before, expressing curiosity as to her identity and commenting on her obvious anxiety. To his surprise the steward became very upset and explained to Sir Walter that he had, in fact, seen a ghost and that her appearance always preceded the death of someone closely associated with the old castle. It appears that the ghost had been seen shortly before his son's death by drowning, and nothing Sir Walter could say would convince the man that his wife too, despite her vastly improved condition, would not die. In the event, the woman did die quite suddenly a few hours later.

So, who was the beautiful and mysterious ghost? Apparently she is the daughter of a former owner of Berry Pomeroy Castle who was as wicked and cruel as she was beautiful. Because of her many crimes and licentious living, she was doomed after her death to haunt forever the scene of some of her evil deeds. Even today there is an appalling sense of loneliness and dread, even of stark evil, around the castle which is often felt by visitors. Some claim to have been lured by a strange urge to an unsafe spot in or near the castle where, but for the presence of mind of others, they would have had a serious accident.

One of the most persistent experiences here over the last fifty years or so is that of the definite sound of a baby's cries, and on occasion the cause of the pitiful sounds is seen. The baby, an illegitimate child, was murdered soon after it was born, by the mother, believed to be another Pomeroy daughter. It is this woman, dressed in a long blue cloak with a hood, that has been witnessed several times close to some arches near the gatehouse. In the mid-1960s a man visiting the castle, who had no knowledge of the haunting or of the infanticide, which took place several hundred years ago, said that the feeling of absolute desolation in the arches where the spectre has been seen was overpowering.

Yet another well-known ghost at Berry Pomeroy Castle, is a third lady owner, Eleanor de Pomeroy. She and her sister Margaret both loved the same man, and Lady Eleanor was so jealous of her beautiful sister that she had her imprisoned in the castle dungeons, where she was starved to death. Now it is said that on certain nights she rises from her dungeon, leaves St Margaret's Tower in flowing white robes and walks the ramparts, beckoning to those unfortunate enough to see her.

In 1968 the castle's curator was given photographs by two separate groups of visitors which show in one print the ghost-like figure of a man in a tricorn hat, and in the other the profile of a beautiful young women. Both these photographs had been taken near the entrance to St Margaret's Tower and the dungeon where Margaret de Pomeroy was incarcerated.

*

Rochester Castle in Kent was designed by Gundulph the Good. Built in 1098, it has seen many stirring moments in the history of England.

On Good Friday 1264 the Earl of Leicester, Simon de Montfort, besieged the castle, which was defended by a Crusader called Ralph de Capo. Inside the castle with de Capo was the beautiful Lady Blanche de Warenne, who was betrothed to marry him. It so happened that one of the men under the command of Simon de Montfort was a knight called Sir Gilbert Clare, a man of guile and cunning and a rejected suitor of Lady Blanche. When eventually the siege was raised, Ralph de Capo left Rochester Castle to pursue the retreating rebels, and Gilbert Clare, seizing the opportunity, disguised himself with a suit of armour resembling that worn by de Capo and entered the castle.

Inside he sought out Lady Blanche, high up on the southern battlements, watching the flight of de Montfort and his men. Looking back at his castle, de Capo saw his lady struggling with the man he knew to be his enemy and, being an archer of some repute, seized a longbow and arrow from one of his men and sent an arrow speeding towards the stranger who was molesting his beloved. The arrow sped true and found its mark, but unfortunately it glanced off the armour Sir Gilbert wore and pierced the heart of Lady Blanche, killing her instantly.

According to contemporary reports, on that same night the ghost of Lady Blanche walked the battlements in a white robe, her black hair streaming behind her, the fatal arrow still embedded in her chest. Still, on the anniversary of her death, she is said to haunt the battlement of the old castle, bewailing the sad fate of having been killed by her lover. There are several versions of what actually happened all those years ago, but the fact remains that her ghost has been seen several times in recent years, and odd happenings, including unexplained footsteps in this part of the ruin, all add to the theory that Lady Blanche de Warenne did die a violent death.

Historic Ludlow Castle in Shropshire was the last fortress on the Welsh border to surrender to Cromwell in 1646. It had long been the seat of the Lords President of Wales until it began to fall into decline following the surrender. Like Rochester Castle, this eleventh-century ruin has long been the haunt of a ghostly White Lady who met death through the cunning of a man. It is also the site of a mysterious 'breathing' noise.

The White Lady is thought to date back to the time of King Henry II, when, during a border clash with Welsh brigands, a young woman, Marion de la Bruyère, was amongst the few retainers left at the castle in the absence of Joce de Dinan, its custodian. Marion had an admirer who was attached to the Welsh enemies of the castle, and she was in the habit of lowering a rope, whenever the opportunity arose, to enable the errant knight to visit her boudoir at night. However, on this occasion he did not come alone, and while he dallied with Marion, he left the rope dangling. Within a very short time, over a hundred Welshmen had swarmed into the castle, and Ludlow was in the hands of the enemy.

Realizing she had been betrayed, Marion took her lover's sword and slew him, before throwing herself from the top of the battlements of the Hanging Tower and crashing to her death on the jagged rocks below.

For many years the ghost of Marion was said to have been seen in the vicinity of the Hanging Tower, wandering aimlessly amongst the ruins on dark nights. Today, all that seems to remain is a curious gasping sound that seems to come from about half-way up the Hanging Tower and is thought to be the last gasps of the knight who betrayed the innocent Marion.

During the Second World War, an evacuated Liverpool family spent several weeks living in part of Ludlow Castle. They had been there only a short time when some strange things began to happen: raps and bangs which could not be accounted for and the mysterious opening and closing of doors. Recent enquiries have revealed that, even as I write, officials are still getting reports of odd happenings in and around the castle, and they also receive complaints of 'wheezing' noises from the Hanging Tower!

Hampton Court, the beautiful palace by the River Thames at Middlesex presented to King Henry VIII by his disgraced Chancellor, Cardinal Thomas Wolsey, has many ghosts both royal and common. Here the great architect Sir Christopher Wren lived during the years he was supervising the renovation work at the palace, and here he died on 26 February 1723.

The palace is known to be haunted still, by the spirit of King Henry VIII's fifth wife, Catherine Howard, beheaded in 1542. She has been seen so frequently, running screaming to the chapel door in search of sanctuary, that she is now officially mentioned in the guide-books issued to tourists. Catherine came here in 1540, a lovely teenaged girl, as bride of the fat, lame and ageing monarch. After little more than a year, ugly rumours began to circulate which suggested she had behaved little better than a common harlot, before and after her marriage.

The night she was arrested – her first step to the block – she broke free of her captors and sped along the gallery in a vain attempt to plead with the King for her life. But the wily old fox sat piously listening to vespers in the chapel and ignored her pleas to open the door. She was dragged away, still shrieking and sobbing for mercy. This grisly event is re-enacted by her ghost on the night of the anniversary of the event, running shrieking through what is now known as the Haunted Gallery.

About a century ago this gallery was used as a store for pictures and was not open to the public, although the adjoining rooms were occupied by an elderly duchess as a 'grace and favour' apartment. She reported that once, in the dead of night, she was wakened by an ear-splitting shriek which died away into a pulsating silence. Earlier this century, when the gallery was opened to the public, an artist was startled to see a ringed hand repeatedly appear in front of the picture he was sketching. Hurriedly he drew the hand and ring and the large jewel which it contained. Later this was identified as one known to have been worn by Queen Catherine Howard.

Another wife of Bluff King Hal, Jane Seymour, has also been seen at Hampton Court Palace. It was here on 12 October 1537, that she, his third Queen, bore Henry a son – later to become King Edward VI – and died a week later. Her ghost has since been seen emerging from the Queen's apartments carrying a lighted taper. She then walks around the Silver Stick Gallery, usually on the anniversary of the birth of her son. In quite recent years members of the staff have handed in their resignation after seeing what they described as 'a tall lady, with a long train and a shiny face', walking through closed doors holding a taper and gliding down the stairs.

When Jane Seymour died, the week after Edward was born, the weakling boy, crowned for a short reign at the age of ten, was fostered by a nurse, Mistress Sibell Penn, whose ghost also appears at Hampton Court. As she watched over the sickly child, the sound of her voice and the whirr of her spinning-wheel would have been some of the first sounds the young prince heard. In fact, Edward never forgot his old nurse; nor did his sisters, Mary and Elizabeth, who granted her a pension and apartments at Hampton Court.

In 1568, whilst staying here, both Mistress Penn and Queen Elizabeth caught smallpox, and although Elizabeth survived, marked for the rest of her life, Mistress Penn was not so fortunate and she died on 6 November of that year. She was buried at nearby St Mary's Church, which was struck by lightning in 1829 and had to be re-built. Sibell Penn's tomb was removed to the new church along with her monument, but her grave was rifled and her remains were scattered.

It was not long after this before strange whirring sounds and mutterings were heard coming from behind a wall at the Palace – a wall behind which there was no known room. When the wall was knocked down, a spinning-wheel was uncovered, along with other relics which indicated that the nurse had once lived here. Some weeks later, a sentry outside this apartment saw a female figure, clad in a long grey robe and hood, emerging from the former rooms of Mistress Penn and vanish before his astonished eyes. Another sentry fled when he saw the phantom pass through a wall. Both men stated later that they had recognized the figure as that of the former nurse by her resemblance to her stone effigy.

Princess Frederica of Hanover, who knew nothing of the phantom nurse, came face to face with her tall, gaunt figure, dressed in a long grey robe with a hood over her head. Her long hands were outstretched before her. Since then, the well-authenticated ghost of Mistress Penn has been known as 'the Lady In Grey'.

Two male figures once haunted Hampton's Fountain Court,

making loud noises in the middle of the night. The ghosts were never seen or heard again after two workmen laying new drains uncovered the skeletons of two young men in Cavalier dress, buried two feet beneath the courtyard. It is thought that the extremely well-preserved remains were those of Lord Francis Villiers and a brother Royalist officer who were killed in a sharp skirmish between King Charles' forces and those of Parliament. Once they had been given a decent Christian burial, the noisy disturbances ceased.

But perhaps the most bizarre phantoms of Hampton Court were those encountered by a police constable on duty at the palace during the First World War. The officer opened a gate in the grounds for two men and seven women wearing strange old-fashioned clothes. He later swore that they had walked on for about thirty yards, turned to one side of the path – and simply faded away.

Today HM The Queen and her immediate family have given over to the nation Hampton Court Palace and its ghosts to the thousands of tourists who visit it every year.

Arundel Castle in Sussex stands on what are believed to be the twelfth-century remains and foundations of a previous castle and has for many centuries been the ancestral home of the dukes of Norfolk, but although the present building might appear medieval, it is in fact mainly nineteenth-century. The castle's ghosts, however, are authentic enough; and there are four of them: a girl, a boy, a seventeenth-century dandy and a white bird.

Arundel Castle is first mentioned in the will of Alfred the Great and came into the hands of the dukes of Norfolk when the third Duke, an uncle of King Henry VIII's fifth wife, Catherine Howard, took possession in 1580. It has remained in the hands of the Norfolk family ever since.

The great kitchen at the castle is said to be haunted by the ghost of a former kitchen boy, who was badly treated by the head cellarer a couple of hundred years ago. Because of the ill-treatment he received, the boy died whilst quite young, and since then his ghost has been heard and seen, cleaning pots and pans as if his spectral life depended on it, long after the rest of the kitchen staff have gone off to bed.

The ghost's female counterpart, a young girl dressed in white, has been seen on still moonlit nights, in the vicinity of Hiorne's Tower, just on the brow of a hill. A tragic story of unrequited love is said to be the cause of the girl's throwing herself off the tower in desperation.

The phantom white bird, a bird of ill-fortune, flutters against the windows of the castle, when the death of one of the Howard family is imminent and there are still those amongst the family retainers who claim to have witnessed this bird, just before the death of the last Duke of Norfolk.

The ghost of the dandy is thought to date back to the days of King Charles II. Known as 'the Blue Man', he is often seen at night dressed in blue silk, poring over old books in the castle library. Just what he is looking for, or why he can never find it, no one really knows. Perhaps he is associated in some way with the sounds of Cromwell's cannon, heard from time to time battering the ramparts of the castle, as they did some 340 years ago, under the command of Sir William Waller.

To visit the last two castles in this chapter, we must travel to the industrial north-east of England, where haunted spots in both town and village are not hard to find. Most are half forgotten, and the restless phantoms appear to terrify the folk less frequently than they once did. However, the disturbing events which were once a terror to those who experienced them were recorded by local historians of days gone by and, in a later age, when modern ghosts replaced older ones, by reporters in local newspapers. One such ghost – that of the Grey Man of Bellister – which haunted the vicinity of Bellister Castle in Northumberland, was sufficiently horrific to be remembered not only in the neighbourhood but throughout the whole of the North-East.

The story goes that one dark night a tired and wandering minstrel sought refuge at Bellister Castle. He was admitted, given food and warmth and offered a bed for the night in accordance with the chivalrous rules upheld by the proud lords of Bellister. After the meal the minstrel, an aged and slightly senile musician, regaled the lord and assembly with an ancient tale, accompanied by the music of his lute. As the hours stretched into morning and most of the company had

32

retired, the tired minstrel withdrew, leaving the lord alone in the great hall.

Sitting alone and reflecting on the day's events, suspicion slowly darkened the lord's thoughts. At the time he was engaged in a feud with a neighbouring baron who was quite adept at the use of cunning and would not be above the employment of subterfuge to gain his own ends. The old lord then began to consider that the minstrel was probably a spy, seeking his hospitality at the castle to obtain a traitorous advantage for his enemy.

The lord allowed his thoughts to build up until he became consumed with an unreasonable and insane rage. Suddenly he rose, awoke the sleeping servants and retainers and ordered them to drag the minstrel from his couch. But it was too late: the old musician had resumed his journey and had left the castle. This discovery only seemed to heighten the lord's suspicions, and a pursuit was quickly organized, the horses were hastily saddled and bloodhounds released on the old musician's trail. They caught up with him on the banks of the River Tyne, where the hounds almost tore the defenceless old man to pieces before the arrival of the lord and his servants, who were too late to prevent the terrible outrage.

Neither remorse nor repentance could efface the deed of violence from the mind of the old lord. Thereafter he was haunted by the terrible memory and by the ghost of the minstrel, who persisted in wandering through the grounds and the castle, a dreadful spectre, its ancient features terribly gashed and blood running into the white beard, a terrifying sight to all who were to see it.

Today the same ghost is seen on rare occasions and is dreaded by all who live in the neighbourhood, for it is said to be a precursor of doom to all who are unfortunate enough to see it.

Finally, Featherstone Castle, an ancient ivy-clad pile beside the South Tyne. It comprises a medieval pele tower and a modernized Jacobean mansion and exudes the atmosphere of chivalry and romance of an age long past. A rather unusual and interesting ghost story is attached to the place which is almost forgotten but for its presentation in local guide-books and histories.

Centuries ago, a baron – a man of exceptional power and character, determination and pride – lived here. He would tolerate no interference with whatever course of action he pursued with determination. He had a young and beautiful daughter and had set his heart on seeing her married only to someone of his own choice, a man equal to himself in riches and power. Unfortunately the man chosen was scarcely attractive in disposition and character, and an unfair match for a gentle and modest maiden.

Now, the baron's daughter not only rebelled against her father's wishes, detesting the proposed husband, but had secretly promised herself to a young knight of equal birth and fortune. Still her tears and pleas were to no avail, and in due course the preparations for the nuptials were completed, the marriage of the unhappy bride took place, music and merriment echoed about the walls of the castle, and the bride and groom left with a group of guests for an evening ride through the nearby forest, to return later to a splendid, mouth-watering banquet in the great hall of Featherstone Castle.

Slowly evening passed into night, and the baron found himself sitting alone by the huge fire, anxiously awaiting the return of his daughter, her husband and the numerous guests. But the hour grew later, the moon rode higher and owls hooted about the castle walls, and yet there was no sign of the party who were to join in the sumptuous banquet and merrymaking. The baron grew restless and paced the great hall in impatience; the minstrels fretted in the gallery, and even the lackeys and cooks became anxious. At length the baron, who was now beside himself, sent out riders in search of the missing party. They returned after some considerable time but with neither word nor explanation, and it was whispered that the wedding party had fallen foul of robbers. According to local historians, this supposition was not all that far from the truth.

The party did return, but not in flesh and blood. They returned as phantoms, for suddenly the night's silence was broken by the sounds of horses and jingling harness, the great door opened and silently in walked the bridegroom, his bride and their friends and guests. Not a sound did their footsteps make. Each took his place at the heavily laden table, grimly and silently, and the baron, who sat petrified in horror, suddenly realized that he was in the company of the dead.

The party had indeed gone riding following the wedding ceremony, and they had been waylaid in the gorge known as Pinkyn Clough by a band of determined men, led by the unhappy and frustrated lover. A furious fight then ensued, during which a thrust made by the unhappy young man was deflected. By a cruel twist of fate, the blade pierced the heart of the young bride, and she fell dead on the spot. The remainder of the party from the castle were soon overcome and slain and thus returned to the festivities as ghosts.

Old traditions die hard and although, to my knowledge, the phantom cavalcade has not been seen for some time now, the story is still told in the cottages in the vicinity, beside the warm fire on cold, dark winter evenings.

2. Those Ladies in Grey

Visitors to Old England are well catered for when it comes to stately homes, halls and country houses, several of which have their resident Grey or White Lady who, although long dead, seem to be some of the commonest kinds of wraith. In many cases the reasons behind the hauntings have been lost in the mists of time, or the details have been distorted in the re-telling. Even the identity of the ghost in question is often shrouded in mystery or in a mixture of fact and fantasy. Many of the stories are no doubt true and have been well authenticated, whilst others leave us in some doubt.

But these old houses do have atmosphere, and whether they be in ruins or are complete, with long passages, oak-panelled rooms and the like, it is not surprising that they acquire a ghost or two. The rest is left to the imagination, which in many instances needs very little encouragement.

One such place is Lorton Hall, near Cockermouth in Cumbria, where the Scots king Malcolm III is said to have stayed with his consort during a progress of the kingdom, back in the eleventh century. Lorton Hall has all the ingredients of a good ghost story. There are a number of priests' hides and a Grey Lady who is seen quite often by visitors to the Hall and who is thought to be the ghost of Elizabeth, the mongoloid daughter of the Bragg family, the original owners of the estate.

It appears that, as Elizabeth grew older, so her mental state grew worse, and when she died, in the late eighteenth century – possibly in her mid-sixties – she would no doubt have been classified as a lunatic. This is borne out to some extent by the fact that there is no record of her burial in the local churchyard, the theory being that the vicar refused to allow lunatics to be buried in consecrated ground.

As her affliction would suggest, Elizabeth's ghostly appearances are always connected with the full moon when, in the early hours of the morning, doors are heard to open and close by themselves and a grey figure, carrying a lighted candle, is often seen drifting down a corridor and passing through the closed dining-room window – which incidentally was the original front door. She was seen by the owners of Lorton as recently as 1972.

The local people who claim to have seen the ghost roaming the grounds of the Hall simply accept her as a fact of life. At the end of the Second World War a company of Girl Guides camping in the grounds were packing up their belongings to return home in the early hours of the morning when several of them together saw the ghostly figure come out of the front door and drift across the grounds.

In 1923 an attempt was to have been made to exorcise the phantom, but on the morning it was to have taken place the priest who was to carry out the exorcism collapsed and died. This was taken as a warning that nothing should be done to interfere with Elizabeth's early morning wanderings, and to this day no further attempts have been made.

In the gardens of the Hall is an unmarked grave which many people believe to be the last resting-place of Elizabeth Bragg. On numerous occasions people have reported seeing the dark figure of a woman standing beside it. One woman on seeing it is said to have been so terrified that she ran to her car, with the intention of driving away, but was so frightened that she crashed, severely damaging the vehicle but fortunately receiving no personal injury. Such is the influence of Elizabeth Bragg.

Still in Cumbria, we find the most complete Tudor House in the whole of the north-west of England – Levens Hall, near Kendal. It is a treasure-house of some fine musical instruments, where every room is panelled with decorative ceilings.

Beautiful as the house is, perhaps its main attraction is the magnificent garden, designed by Guillaume Beaumont and laid out between 1689 and 1705. Other attractions are the ghosts that are seen quite frequently on the premises but about whom not a lot is known.

Recently I had the pleasure of interviewing the owners of Levens Hall for a television series, and Mrs Robin Bagot, mother of Hal Bagot, the present owner, told me that she had frequently seen the ghost of a woman in a long pink dress and mob cap. Although her identity is not known for sure, it is thought she might be the ghost of a housekeeper. She once scared the life out of a group of Women's Institute members who saw her at the top of the stairs whilst visiting the house in 1972. One fascinating aspect regarding this ghost is an old patchwork quilt made of the pink material of the gown which the lady is seen wearing.

But the most often sighted and best-known phantom of Levens Hall is the Grey Lady seen quite recently. This is thought to be the ghost of a gypsy who in the seventeenth century was turned away from the Hall when begging for food. Before dying of starvation, she cursed the family living there at the time, saying that 'no son would inherit the house until the River Kent ceased to flow and a white fawn was born'. Strange as it may seem, history relates that this prophesy came true – until fate took a hand to ensure the curse was lifted. For when Alan Bagot was born, the river froze solid and a white deer was seen shortly afterwards amongst the herd, thus heralding a new era. To prove it, the fawn's ears have been preserved at the Hall.

The Grey Lady, though, continued to haunt the grounds of the Hall. She was seen in 1971 by the seven-year-old daughter of Mrs Bagot, walking across a field and going right through a small shed which had been erected for her daughter's pony. The child described her in great detail, even though she was too young to realize that the woman was dressed in the clothes of a seventeenth-century peasant. Again in 1971, she was seen standing on a narrow bridge leading to the house, when she nearly caused a nasty car accident, averted only by the skill of the driver.

Another Grey Lady who makes life difficult for passing motorists can be met on the A677 road, just about half-way between Preston and Blackburn in Lancashire. Here, brooding alongside the road, stands Samlesbury Hall, built during the reign of Edward III with oak from the surrounding primeval forests, being selected for the massive timbers which form the framework of this lovely old building.

The original Samlesbury Hall stood for about 200 years, a mile or so from the present building, by a ford over the River Ribble and was built during the reign of King Henry II, by Gospatrick de Samlesbury. Following the Scots victory at Bannockburn, David Bruce raided south Lancashire in about 1332, attacking and destroying the old Hall. A few years later the inheritance passed through marriage to Gilbert de Southworth of Winwick, who decided to re-build Samlesbury Hall in its present position, because of the ever-present threat from Scottish raiding parties. Work began in 1340, and the Hall remained in the hands of the Southworth family for the next 350 years. Unfortunately they had the unhappy knack of throwing their weight behind the wrong causes, and through this and heavy fines, which severely strained the family purse-strings, they were eventually forced to sell their lands. Since then the Hall has had many uses. It has been in turn a private residence, an inn and a girls' boarding-school. Today it is restored to its former glory and has been opened up to the public.

The well-known haunting of Samlesbury Hall goes back to the sixteenth century and old Sir John Southworth. One of his daughters, Dorothy, fell in love with the heir of a neighbouring knightly, but Protestant, family. Sir John was enraged that his daughter should even contemplate marrying the son of a family who had deserted the Roman Catholic faith, and he forbade the young man to go anywhere near his daughter again. Unfortunately Sir John's wrath only served to make the young couple all the more determined to marry, and after many secret meetings they agreed to elope. However, the time and place were overheard by one of the girl's brothers who was hiding in the bushes nearby and who was determined to prevent his sister's disgracing the family name.

On the night the couple planned to elope, they met at the pre-arranged hour and, as the knight moved away with his bride-to-be, her brother rushed from his hiding-place and slew him and the two friends who were helping them. Their bodies were secretly buried near the domestic chapel at the Hall, and Lady Dorothy was sent abroad to a convent, where she is said to have gone mad and died, shortly afterwards. Last century, when the new turnpike road was being built – the A677 – three skeletons were discovered in a shallow grave near the walls of the Hall, which has helped to strengthen the tradition ever since.

Now, on still, clear evenings, the ghostly figure of a woman in white can be seen, passing along the corridors and the gallery, then out into the grounds. About thirty years ago, when a play telling of the tragedy of the Southworth family was staged in the Great Hall, a member of the cast saw a lady in white crossing the grounds; no member of the cast had left the Hall during this time. During the Second World War, two soldiers met the White Lady as they returned to their hut in the grounds late one night, and I know of one caretaker's daughter who told of waking one night to find someone leaning over her bed. Another woman has seen the lady in white passing along the corridors, and some people who sat up all night to watch for her were rewarded by the sounds of weeping and the rustling of skirts and saw a chair rocking of its own accord.

In the 1970s a bus passing on the main road towards Blackburn actually stopped for her, the driver taking her for a late-night passenger; and in 1981 a wholesale fruiterer was driving past the Hall at about 4.30 in the morning and braked hard when the figure of a woman, dressed in a flowing white dress, drifted out of the grounds and in front of his vehicle.

Speke Hall, near Liverpool Airport, was for over 500 years the home of the Norris family, which provided the country with many soldiers and statesmen. They also gave the Hall a haunted room, a ghostly apparition and an empty cradle which, even today, is rocked by invisible hands.

In Tudor times the Norrises were very active in demolishing and re-building, the present Hall (little of which is changed today) being completed during the reign of King Henry VIII. Like most of their neighbours, the Norrises refused to change their religion during the period of persecution of Roman Catholics under the Tudors, and in spite of great pressures being brought to bear they remained loyal to their faith. Because of its position at Speke, with a nearby ford across the River Mersey, the Hall became an active Mass-centre and a reception- and departure-point for priests and other Catholics fleeing for their lives. It is riddled with hides and secret rooms which were well used during the Elizabethan era, the panelled walls concealing hidden chambers and escape passages which run all around the Hall.

During the reign of the Catholic Queen Mary and later under King James I, the Norris family received many royal favours, which they returned by supporting King Charles I in the Civil War. The last of the male line died following the Restoration of the monarchy in 1660, leaving as sole heir his daughter Mary, who later married one Lord Sidney Beauclerk, a self-styled literary gentleman and patron of the arts, who counted among his friends Samuel Johnson and the painter Sir Joshua Reynolds. Beauclerk was not a very good husband, and he caused Mary so much unhappiness that she is said to have ended her life and that of her son, Topham, by throwing herself, child in arms, into the moat.

It is said to be poor Mary's ghost which now haunts the Hall, and her hands which still rock the child's cradle quite regularly, all these centuries later. There is, however, some doubt as to the real identity of the Speke Hall ghost, for it is thought by historians to be highly unlikely that the Beauclerks actually lived there. However, there is no doubt that one of the rooms, the tapestry room, is haunted, and quite a few people have reported a presence here. The cradle has often been seen rocking, and an apparition has been seen in one of the bedrooms, where it disappears into a wall near the window. Recent examination has brought to light a concealed entrance to a passage just here, which leads down through an outside wall.

A few miles to the north-east of Speke, in the flat countryside about seven miles from Ormskirk, on the A59 Preston road, stands Rufford Old Hall, a fifteenth-century manor house believed to have been built on the site of an older house and which has been altered twice since the days of Robert Hesketh who built the Manor and held it until 1490. Today the Hall comprises the original Great Hall of timber construction, a brick wing, added about 1660, and an intervening section dating from the early nineteenth century. It was presented to the National Trust by the late Lord Hesketh in 1936.

Tradition has it that the young William Shakespeare once performed at the Hall. Indeed, there is documentary evidence to show that one 'William Shakeshaft' was a member of the Hesketh players who visited Rufford around 1584. This does, in fact, coincide with Shakespeare's absence from Stratford after allegedly stealing deer from Charlecote Park.

Like most families in the area, the Heskeths were Catholics, and their beliefs were to cause them quite a lot of grief during the persecutions. Priests were harboured at Rufford: above a canopy in the Great Hall, a secret chamber is concealed, part of its clay floor remaining in position. This chamber was discovered only in 1949, and it is believed to have been constructed during the religious strife in the second half of the sixteenth century.

There is a well-authenticated ghost of a lady in grey at the Hall, who is seen quite often and quite clearly in the grounds, her form solid-looking, though she casts no shadow. This Grey Lady is thought by many to be the ghost of a member of the Hesketh family whose husband was called away to fight in some obscure Scottish war soon after their wedding. Some time later, she was told by a soldier passing through the village that her husband was on his way back home. In vain the poor girl waited, but her husband never came. She refused her food and in time was taken to her bed, where her condition gradually deteriorated and she died. It is said that on her death-bed she promised that her spirit would stay on at the Hall to await her lover's return.

Another ghost, said to be that of Queen Elizabeth I, has also been reported seen in the dining-room on at least two occasions. However, as there is no record of the Queen's ever having stayed at Rufford Old Hall, this ghost cannot really be authenticated. Still, who knows? Good Queen Bess is always said to be popping up in some remote country house or another.

To reach the Brontë village of Haworth, most tourists travel through the woollen-manufacturing town of Keighley, only about four miles from Haworth in West Yorkshire. Within a few yards of the busy A560 Keighley-Bradford road stands East Riddlesden Hall, a seventeenth-century manor house built by the Rishworth family. The Hall is known to be haunted by an unidentified lady wearing a long blue dress which can be heard swishing about as she walks aimlessly along corridors and in and out of rooms. Here too they have a child's cradle which has been seen rocking, without the aid of human hands.

Mr M. Atkins, now living in Whitby, used to be a taxi-driver in Keighley and he related an interesting experience at the Hall in December 1963, when he was called there to pick up a fare. He told me, 'There is a large stone porch, and when I got there it was quite dark with no lights either in the porch or in the grounds. I couldn't find the bell-push in the dark, so I went round and peered through one of the windows nearby.' He was surprised to see, inside the room, a lady in period dress, but as it was very near Christmas he assumed there must be a fancy-dress party going on. Going back to the door, he found it was not locked, so he let himself into the large reception hall. There was no one about, which seemed rather strange if there was a party going on, and the place was as quiet as a church, except for some music coming faintly from somewhere down a long passage. Following the sound, he found himself in the caretaker's room, where there was a lady waiting for him to take her home in his taxi.

Mr Atkins continued, 'In the taxi I said to the lady that I thought there was a party going on and told her what I had seen through the window. She sat quiet for some time and then she said, "Do you know you have seen our ghost."' He told me later that he really didn't believe in ghosts, but one thing he did know: that woman was there in the Hall all right. Had Mr Atkins seen the mysterious 'Lady in Blue'? If so, who was she? Was she a member of the Rishworth family, or was she a nanny, who, like so many unfortunate young women before and since, met with a tragic end?

Another anonymous Grey Lady haunts Bolling Hall at Bradford, twelve miles south-east of Keighley. The ghost which haunts this beautiful old manor house was thought to

have been responsible for saving the lives of the whole
population of Bradford during the English Civil War.

In 1643 the Hall was owned by Richard Tempest, an ardent
supporter of King Charles I, and it was beneath his roof that
the Earl of Newcastle stayed the night after issuing the grim
orders for the massacre of every man, woman and child in
Bradford. The town was a hotbed of Puritanism and lay
under siege by the King's forces. The Earl of Newport had
been killed during the laying of the siege, and Newcastle was
so incensed by this that he issued the now infamous order that
on the following day his soldiers should 'put to the sword every
man, woman and child, without regard to age or distinction
whatsoever'.

That night the Earl slept badly – he reported that three
times the clothes were pulled from his bed and a ghostly
female form had appeared, dressed all in white, which appealed
to him in 'piteous and lamentable tones' to 'pity poor
Bradford'. Sceptics said the Earl was drunk. Others were not
quite so polite and suggested the female was not a ghost but a
venturesome wench who lived nearby. Who, or whatever, it
was, succeeded in persuading the Earl to cancel the previous
day's order and thus spare the citizens of Bradford.

A resident in Bradford at the time of the siege, Joseph
Lister, was to write later, 'It was generally reported that
something came on the Lord's Day night and pulled the
clothes off his bed many times.'

Visitors to Willington, a Northumberland village situated
about five miles west of South Shields at the mouth of the River
Tyne, will stumble across some old buildings near the riverside
which were formerly a millhouse and where, over a century ago,
a staunch Quaker, Joseph Proctor, and his family first
experienced what was to become one of the most important and
amongst the best documented hauntings in the country.

When the Proctor family moved into the millhouse in about
1834, they paid little attention to rumours that the place was
haunted. The house was a pleasant and comparatively new
building set by the river, in what was then a rugged part of the
country. They were a respectable Quaker family, and Joseph
Proctor was said to have been a man of high intelligence and

common sense, and like all Quakers he was a good and kind husband and father who treated his employees well. Yet within ten years the Proctors were driven to leave in distress, unable to stand any more of the weird and ghostly happenings that plagued them from the day they first arrived at Willington Mill. It was only some years later that they were to discover that their house had been built on the site of an old cottage where, years before, a terrible crime had been committed and a priest had refused to hear the dying confession of a woman who wanted to unburden herself.

The first recorded incidents at Willington Mill for which no normal explanation could be found began one night in January 1835. A young nursemaid was putting the children to bed in the second-floor nursery when she heard curious noises, sounding like a dull, heavy tread of footfalls, coming from the room above. The noises came from an empty room never used by the family and sounded like someone pacing backwards and forwards for about ten minutes. At first the girl took no notice, thinking they must be the footsteps of one of the handymen with a job to do, but they went on night after night, getting louder all the time. Other servants and members of the family also heard them, but when they burst into the room to surprise the 'intruder', no one was there. Sometimes people sat in the room or occupied it all night, but no cause for the noise was discovered and it was seemingly impossible that the sounds could have been made by trickery.

One morning, while Mr Proctor was conducting family worship, suddenly the heavy steps were heard coming down the stairs, past the parlour and along the hall to the front door. The family and their servants all heard the sound of the bar being removed, two bolts drawn back and the lock turned. Mr Proctor rushed into the hall to find the door wide open and the 'invisible' footsteps going down the path. Mrs Proctor fainted on the spot.

After a very short time it became difficult to keep servants. The only one who loyally refused to leave was Mary Young, who had come with the family from their previous home in North Shields.

Next came a period when it seemed the whole house had been taken over by unseen people. There were sounds of doors opening, people entering and leaving rooms, thumps, blows and laboured breathing, the steps of a child, chairs being moved and the delicious rustle of a woman in a silk dress hurrying by. The haunting remained entirely one of sounds, until one Whitsuntide, when Mary Young was washing dishes in the kitchen, she heard footsteps in the passage and, on looking up, saw a woman in a lavender silk dress go upstairs and enter one of the rooms. That night the noises in the house were louder than they had been at any other time, and no one got any sleep.

Two of Mrs Proctor's sisters arrived for a visit. On their very first night, sleeping together in the same four-poster bed, they felt it lift up. Their first reaction was that there was a thief hidden there, so they rang the alarm, and the men of the house came running. Nothing was found. On another night their bed was violently shaken and the curtains were suddenly hoisted up, then let down again, several times. They got up and removed the curtains and then, lying half-awake, were suddenly horrified when a misty, bluish figure of a woman drifted out of the wall and leaned over them in an almost horizontal position. Both sisters saw the figure quite clearly and lay, speechless with fright, as it retreated and passed back into the wall. After that neither of them would sleep in the room another night, and one of them was so afraid that she even left the house to take lodgings with the mill foreman and his family.

One dark, moonless night, when the mill foreman and his wife were walking past the mill after paying a call on neighbours, they watched fascinated as a luminous figure, which appeared to be dressed in 'priestly garments', glided back and forth at the height of the second floor. It seemed to glide through the outer wall of the house and then stand looking out of the window at them.

The focus of the haunting seemed to be in what the Proctors called 'the Blue Room', and in the summer of 1840 they agreed to let a psychic investigator, Edward Drury, spend a night there. Drury took along a friend to assist, who refused to sleep in the bed but agreed to sit up and doze in an armchair. Drury was later to describe what happened. He said that he looked at his watch at ten minutes to one in the morning and as he looked up he distinctly saw the closet door open and the figure of a woman in greyish garments, her head inclined downwards and one hand clutching her chest as if in pain, advance with a cautious step across the floor towards him. The figure, on approaching his friend asleep in the chair, extended its right hand towards him. At that moment, Drury rushed at it ...

It was over three hours before Drury could recollect anything more. He had been carried downstairs in a state of terror by Mr Proctor, all the time shrieking, 'There she is. Keep her off. For God's sake, keep her off!' Afterwards the Grey Lady was seen more frequently. So were unearthly animals and other startling apparitions.

Although the Proctors tried to shield their children from the worst of the hauntings, they too were to become involved eventually. One day a daughter said to Mary Young, 'There is a lady sitting on the bed in mama's room. She has eye-holes, but no eyes and she looked hard at me.' Then another daughter reported that during the night a lady had come out of the wall and stood looking in the mirror. She had no eyes, although she had eye-holes.

By 1847 Joseph Proctor and his family could endure the hauntings no longer. They moved to another part of Northumberland and were never again troubled by ghosts. The house was later divided into two dwellings and eventually deteriorated into a slum. Although it was never to experience the same terrors the Proctors knew, people continued to see and hear strange things from time to time, and even today the site is still not entirely free from psychic manifestations.

The ghost of a tall woman dressed in grey often mingles with tourists looking over Chambercombe Manor at the seaside resort of Ilfracombe in North Devon. She was seen as recently as 1981, when she was reported to have a smile on her face, which is surprising really, for the story of her life – and death – is far from a happy one.

Alexander Oatway was one of the notorious West Country shipwreckers of the seventeenth century. On wild, stormy nights he would leave the comfort of his fireside at Chambercombe and hurry down to the shore carrying a powerful lantern, which he used as a decoy beacon to lure trusting ships' captains seeking safe harbour onto the dangerous rocks, where he and his friends would plunder the vessels. One wild night Oatway was accompanied by his son William. The lantern trick worked again, except that on this occasion there was a survivor from the wreck, a pretty young Spanish girl. William Oatway rescued her and took her home, and they fell in love. In due course they were married and settled on Lundy Island, in the Bristol Channel, where they were blessed within a year with a daughter, Kate.

We now move on twenty years in time. William Oatway learned that his father had died and his old home, Chambercombe Manor, was vacant and to rent. He decided to move back. There his daughter Kate fell in love with an Irish sea-captain called Wallace, and when they married, Captain Wallace took his bride back to his home in Dublin.

Several more years passed. Then, one winter's night, a vicious storm blew up and William, now back in his old ways of wrecking and looting, hurried down to the beach below Chambercombe Manor after spotting a ship in trouble. He found a woman lying on the rocks, her face badly disfigured after the battering she had taken in the sea. She was carried to the Manor but died during the night. As they checked the dead woman's belongings, William and his wife fell to temptation, for she was carrying a money-belt containing enough money and jewellery to enable them to buy Chambercombe Manor outright.

Two days later an official from the Admiralty called, making enquiries about a missing passenger from the wrecked ship. The Oatways denied any knowledge of her, asking the official her name. They were mortified to learn it was a Mrs Katherine Wallace, late of Dublin!

William and his wife were devastated. They had stolen from their own dead daughter, her face unrecognizable because of the impact of the rocks. Filled with guilt and remorse, they walled up her body in a secret room and quite soon moved out of the Manor and away from the district.

It was to be another 150 years or more before their secret was revealed. In 1865 a farmer living in the house was busy re-thatching the roof when he looked down and saw a skeleton lying on a cramped bed in a room he never knew existed. The walls were taken down and the bones buried in a pauper's grave at Ilfracombe. But the ghost of poor Kate Wallace refuses to leave her childhood home, Chambercombe Manor.

For well over 375 years the ghost of a woman dressed in mourning has been seen wandering the grounds of lovely Bisham Abbey, a delightful manor house near Marlow in Buckinghamshire, seemingly washing her hands in a bowl which moves in front of her. Two schoolboys once reported seeing her in a rowing-boat on the River Thames which flows at the bottom of the manor gardens.

This pathetic spectre is thought to be the ghost of Dame Elizabeth Hoby, wife of a respected scholar and close friend of Queen Elizabeth I. She wrote poetry in both Latin and English, and she was rather over-ambitious for her own children, forever urging them to greater efforts, particularly in their classical studies. But she despaired of her youngest son, William, for not only was he slower but his exercise books were full of grammatical errors, mis-spelt words and, in particular, ink blots. For these sins he was given severe beatings by his mother, but instead of improving his work it only served to make him more slovenly than before.

One morning Dame Elizabeth was more exasperated than usual. She boxed the boy's ears and ordered him to repeat the work he had done so badly, locking him in a cupboard until he had completed the task. Just at that moment a messenger arrived from the Queen. Dame Elizabeth was required at Court immediately. She left in a hurry – and forgot to tell the servants where her youngest son was. Alas, when she returned that evening, the boy was found slumped over his books, dead.

Until her death in 1609 at the age of ninety-one, Dame Elizabeth never forgave herself. In 1840, when workmen moved into the house to carry out repairs and structural alterations, between some Tudor floor joists they found several books with a child's writing in them. One of the pages was blotted – not with ink. The smudges were caused by the long-dried tears which had fallen on the pages over 200 years before.

*

Raynham Hall, about six miles south-west of Fakenham in Norfolk, on the A1065 road, is the seat of the marquesses of Townshend and home of the famous Brown Lady.

According to the best authorities, the ghost is that of Lady Dorothy Townshend who has haunted this stately home for 250 years and once caused considerable fright to King George IV. According to her portrait, she has large, shining eyes and is dressed in brown brocade with yellow trimmings and a ruff around her throat. Indeed, she appears to be a harmless-looking lady of the eighteenth century, when the portrait is viewed by daylight. But viewed by candle-light, her appearance is malevolent, and if the candle-light is thrown on the portrait from certain angles, the flesh appears to shrink from the face and the eyes disappear, giving it the semblance of a skull.

When the portrait was sold with some of the Townshend heirlooms at Christie's in 1904, it was catalogued as *The Brown Lady – Dorothy Walpole, wife of the second and most famous Marquess of Townshend*. If that is true, she must have been the daughter of Robert Walpole, Member of Parliament for nearby Houghton, and sister of the great Sir Robert Walpole, the first Prime Minister of England.

No one knows how she died. Her death may have been due to smallpox, of a broken heart or by falling down Raynham's grand staircase. Whatever the cause, her ghost very soon became the terror of visitors to the Hall and servants alike. She has been seen by dozens of people over the last $2\frac{1}{2}$ centuries and is a well-established ghost, one of the very few to have been photographed *in situ*.

The novelist Captain Marryat, when staying at Raynham in the 1830s, saw the ghost near the room he occupied, which contained the famous portrait. He was walking along the corridor towards his room one evening when he met the apparition, who, he said, 'grinned at me in a diabolical manner'. At the time, he happened to be carrying a pistol, which he discharged at the figure at point-blank range, hoping to prove whether it was a ghost or someone playing a trick. The figure disappeared immediately and the bullet, which he swore passed right through her, was later found embedded in a door, behind which she had appeared.

In 1926 Lady Townshend reported that her son and a friend met the Brown Lady on a stairway; later, when they saw the portrait, they both declared that this was the woman they had met, although at the time they claimed to know nothing about the ghost.

Lady Townshend wanted a series of photographs taken of the interior of Raynham Hall, and she commissioned Mr Indra Shira, a professional photographer, to take them. On the afternoon of 19 September 1936 he and his assistant, Mr Provand, were taking flashlight pictures of the grand staircase, Mr Provand wielding the big plate camera and tripod, whilst Mr Shira stood a little behind him, casting his professional eye over the splendid staircase. Mr Provand took a picture and was putting in another plate and re-setting the flash equipment when Mr Shira, looking up the first flight of stairs, saw what he later described as, 'a vapour-like form, gradually assuming the appearance of a woman, draped and veiled in some diaphanous material'. The figure glided down the staircase with floating steps, and the excited Mr Shira told his companion to get a shot quickly. Here was the making of a sensational picture.

Mr Provand could not see the apparition and he wondered why Mr Shira was so excited. Nevertheless, he aimed his camera at the required spot and took another picture. Later, when Mr Shira told him he had seen the ghost descending the stairs, Mr Provand pooh-poohed the idea, whereupon Mr Shira bet him £5 that a ghost would appear on the plate. Mr Shira won his bet: the Brown Lady had been captured for posterity, although this time she was not in her traditional brown brocade but appeared, though only in outline, as a bride in white, enveloped in a clinging veil.

The photograph was published in the magazine *Country Life* of 16 December 1936, and the original photograph can still be seen in the *Country Life* photographic library. Experts who have examined it and the plate are satisfied that there was no trickery.

However, the fact that she should appear in her wedding gown and not her traditional brown brocade, to pose for Mr Shira and his companion, might be said to lend a little colour to one legend about her – that she had been a beautiful girl of the eighteenth century forced to marry an old lecher against her will and to endure a horrifying wedding night with him. But one cannot say for certain that this photograph *is* of the ghost of the Brown Lady. Perhaps Raynham Hall has two, for whilst ghosts have been known to change their habits, I don't know of any who change their clothes.

For about 200 years the Bank of England, in Threadneedle Street in the City of London, was patrolled by Britain's famous Guardsmen. Their nightly chore was to protect the gold in the Bank's huge vaults, something they had done since the Gordon Riots in the 1780s. Modern security devices made the Guardsmen redundant in 1972, but the Bank's other nightly visitor still makes her rounds of the famous building, as she has for almost 175 years.

She is known as 'the Black Nun', because the many witnesses who have seen her say she wears thick black clothes and a dark veil which hides her face. This apparition is thought to be the ghost of Sarah Whitehead, and she is said to be roaming the building looking for her brother Philip. He had been a clerk at the Bank and in 1811 was arrested and charged with forgery and later convicted and hanged, unknown to his sister.

When Sarah did not hear from her brother for some time, she went to the Bank to enquire after him, and when she was given the news that he had been sent to the gallows, the shock made her go completely insane. The very next morning she was back at the Bank, dressed in black mourning clothes and a thick veil, asking if anyone had seen her brother; and for the next twenty-five years she would walk up and down Threadneedle Street every day, looking for Philip, stopping passers-by and going into the Bank itself.

Her lonely search did not end with the poor woman's death. Shortly after her burial, in the graveyard of St Christopher-le-Stocks, the City church which later became part of the Bank's gardens, the lady in black was seen again and again and soon became something of a legend among the clerks who worked at the Bank. Dozens of them claimed to have seen her still searching for her lost brother, often in the old graveyard gardens, sobbing and pounding a stone slab with her hands.

The Guards and the gold are now gone from the Bank, but the little figure in thick black clothes and dark veil which hides her face still keeps up her search for the brother who, after leaving for his work one morning, never came back home again.

In the famous Sitwell family, it was always known as 'the Renishaw Coffin'. The well-known literary trio – Edith, Osbert and Sacheverell – heard about it when they were young children, and the stories of it and its ghost became a part of their up-bringing.

Their former home, Renishaw Hall, is a dark and gloomy Derbyshire mansion dating from about 1625 and has always been thought to be haunted, but it was not until their eccentric father, Sir George Sitwell, decided to do some alterations to the house and enlarge the central staircase, that the coffin was discovered.

In order for the work to be carried out, two small rooms, one on the ground floor and a first-floor bedroom, had to be demolished. Old Sir George, proud of his family history, told the clerk of works to take note of anything unusual he might come across whilst they were doing the work, in the hope that some traces of the older parts of the building might be found. What could be a more interesting to find than a coffin, discovered between the joists of the bedroom floor? From its construction, plus the fact that instead of screws nails had been used, it was presumed to date from about the seventeenth century. It was firmly fastened to the joists with iron clamps and, because of the lack of space, it had never been fitted with a lid, the floorboards serving admirably for that purpose. The coffin did not contain a skeleton, but marks inside it appeared to bear out the fact that there had once been a body in it.

This discovery was to throw a new light on the frightening experiences of two young ladies who had slept in that small room when they were guests at Renishaw Hall, some years previous. The first was the daughter of the Archbishop of Canterbury, who had been invited to Derbyshire in about 1885 to join a large houseparty celebrating the coming of age of Sir George. In the early hours of the morning she claimed to have been wakened by someone kissing her three times. The kisses were ice-cold! The room was empty! Frightened, the young woman ran to the bedroom where Sir George's sister was sleeping and told her of her experience. Miss Sitwell let her sleep in her bed with her, explaining that nothing would induce *her* to sleep in that room as she had experienced the same thing.

Following the party, Sir George Sitwell's agent came to see him on business, and during later conversation Sir George jokingly told him the story of the Archbishop's daughter's phantom kisses. Far from being amused, the agent was shocked, because it seems that, when Sir George had generously lent him Renishaw Hall for his honeymoon, a friend of the agent's bride had also come to stay. She had slept in that same bedroom and had had exactly the same experience. She left the following morning, obviously frightened, but the agent and his wife had just thought she was being over-imaginative.

One evening, some years after the staircase had been enlarged, Lady Sitwell was entertaining a few guests in the upstairs drawing-room after dinner. The room was brightly lit, and the door to the passage outside the room was open. Chatting to a friend, she became conscious of a figure outside, a figure which she later described as, 'of such distinctiveness I had no doubt at all, that I was looking at a real person'. The figure was that of a woman, apparently a servant, with grey hair tied in a bun under her white cap. Her dress was blue with a full dark skirt. She was moving with a furtive, gliding motion, as if she wanted to avoid being noticed, although her arms were stretched out in front of her and the hands were clasped. She moved towards the head of the enlarged staircase – and simply disappeared.

Lady Sitwell called out, 'Who's that?' When she got no reply, she asked her friends to help her find the mysterious woman. They all joined in the search and were just on the point of giving up when a young woman, looking down into the well-lit hall below, suddenly cried out, 'I do believe that is the ghost!' Just where the door to the old room used to be, she saw a woman with dark hair and dress, obviously distressed and in deep thought. Her figure, though solid, cast no shadow. It moved in a gentle glide, full of sadness and melted away.

54

What had happened in those two rooms Sir **George Sitwell**
had demolished has never been discovered to this day, and the
empty coffin has also kept its grim secret.

Littlecote House, a magnificent Tudor mansion house, stands
off the A4 road, about three miles from Hungerford railway
station in Berkshire. It was built between 1490 and 1520 and
houses many beautiful items of furniture, panelled walls, a
carpet from the Palace of Versailles, a library full of rare and
interesting volumes, Dutch paintings, a collection of armoury
from the English Civil War, a beautiful chapel – and several
ghosts.

The best-known story attached to the house concerns the
Darrell family, who owned the place in Elizabethan times.
'Wild' or 'Wicked' Will Darrell, the black sheep of the family,
is said to have murdered a new-born child here in 1575,
having told the midwife minutes after it was born to throw the
child into the fire. Despite her protests, Darrell grabbed the
baby from her arms and tossed it into the fire, holding the
child down with his boot until the little body was consumed
by the flames.

This charge is based on the midwife's death-bed confession.
She said she was called to the house one dark night, to attend
in secret a lady about to have a child; she was promised a large
sum of money if she would do so. She allowed herself to be
taken blindfolded on horseback to a house she did not
recognize, where she delivered the child, which was then
murdered. The midwife claimed she was too terrified to say
anything at the time, but she had had the presence of mind to
cut off a piece of the bed-hanging and to count the number of
stairs, as she was led out again, blindfolded. Subsequently,
after this confession, suspicion fell on Darrell as the murderer
and Littlecote as the house. In due course he was arrested and
put on trial, but somehow he was acquitted, although local
belief was that the child was his, possibly born to his own
sister.

One day in 1589 Darrell was hunting in Littlecote Park
when the ghost of the murdered child suddenly appeared in
front of him, so startling his horse that he was thrown and his
neck was broken, killing him instantly. To this day, the place

is known as 'Darrell's Stile', and I am told that horses still show fright at this particular spot.

Littlecote House, which is open to the public, is owned by the Wills tobacco family, and in 1927, whilst sleeping in their bedroom near the Long Gallery, Sir Edward Wills and his wife were disturbed by the sound of someone coming up the creaking stairs. Silently Sir Edward slipped out into the passage, where he saw a lady with a lamp in her hand which cast shadows on the ceiling. Her hair was fair, she was not very tall, and she wore what looked like a pink nightdress. Sir Edward followed the figure, which disappeared into the room occupied by his younger brother, George.

From time to time, terrifying screams have been heard in the small hours from the direction of the bedroom and landing that were the scene of the tragedy, and some people claim to have seen the apparition of the grief-stricken mother with a baby in her arms. Others maintain the spot is haunted by the frenzied midwife, a woman dressed in brown. In 1968 a female figure was seen to walk along the narrow passageway, through a doorway on the north side and out into the garden, and in 1969 footsteps were heard by guides in the Long Gallery, long after the public had left. Another guide maintained that she saw a woman standing in the garden who disappeared after a few seconds.

In 1970 a lecturer for the National Trust took some photographs of the four-poster bed in the haunted 'murder room'. I am told that when the film was developed a semi-transparent shape could be seen, leaning through the curtains surrounding the bed. Again, late in 1970, a journalist reported seeing the apparition of a woman with a child in her arms.

3. Dark, Mysterious Gentlemen

For every 'Grey Lady' in the country, there appears to be a spectral male counterpart. The stories behind some of these ghosts may not be as romantic, but in many instances they are equally as tragic. Many are the result of the religious persecutions of the sixteenth century or of the English Civil War, whilst others result from some foul deed committed in the course of some long-forgotten cause. Some seem to have no reason at all behind their continuous hauntings, such as the ghost which haunts Greta Hall.

Greta Hall at Keswick, that Cumbrian gateway to the English Lake District, was built in 1800 by William Jackson in preparation for his retirement. He then divided it and rented a portion to his friend the poet Samuel Coleridge, for £25 a year. Coleridge moved in with his young wife in 1803 and persuaded his brother-in-law, Robert Southey, to move in with them, as Southey and his wife Edith were still mourning the death of their young daughter. This arrangement, thought at the time to be a temporary change of scene for Robert and Edith Southey, became permanent, and they were to stay at Greta Hall for the rest of their lives.

Robert Southey can best be described as 'one of nature's gentlemen'. When, in 1804, the self-indulgent Coleridge deserted his family, it was Southey who took on the responsibility of caring for them. In 1813 he was created Poet Laureate, a title he was to retain until his death in 1843. During his years at Greta Hall, he entertained many notable personages, including Sir Walter Scott, Hazlitt, William and Dorothy Wordsworth, Charles and Mary Lamb and Shelley, to name but a few. Later the Hall was to become part of the junior girls' boarding-house of Keswick school and, as can be imagined, it is still haunted by the benign spirit of Robert Southey.

During the period 1914-18, Mrs Sarah Bowe was in service as a maid at Keswick school, and her duties were confined to Greta Hall, where the girls were accommodated under the care and overall supervision of Mrs Hudson, the wife of the headmaster. During school term Mrs Bowe was kept very busy with the care of the younger children and with other household duties. During the holidays there were house guests and the conducting of visitors around the Hall to take up most of her time.

One night, whilst sleeping alone at the top of the building, during a quiet time of the school holidays, Mrs Bowe left the gas-light turned down low when she went to bed. She awoke later and saw, standing under the gas-lamp, the figure of a man with his back half turned towards her, reading a book. She realized it was the noise of his turning the pages as he read that had disturbed her. There being no one else in the house, she was too terrified to move and just lay as she was until daybreak. When she did pluck up enough courage to look again, the figure had gone. It was not until some time after this, when she came across a likeness of Robert Southey, that she recognized him as her visitor.

Mrs Bowe had not previously been told of any haunting, and when she related her experience to Mrs Hudson, the whole matter was dismissed with Edwardian fervour as 'stuff and nonsense'. However, the story came to the ears of the wife of the French teacher, who, having approached Mrs Bowe and heard her experience again, said, 'Do you remember, Sarah, that some time ago I tried to dissuade you from taking your bath late at night?' She then went on to explain how she had run her bath late one night and, as she settled down into it, she looked up and was horrified to see the figure of a man in his shirtsleeves with his back towards her, looking out of the window.

Stepping quickly out of the bath, the teacher's wife opened the door and ran naked back to her room, screaming for her husband. Apparently several members of the staff heard her screams but had assumed she and her volatile husband were having another of their quarrels.

*

There is a long tradition which connects Charlotte Brontë with the hamlet of Wycoller, about 6½ miles west of her home at Haworth. Each year thousands of Brontë-lovers come here in search of the Brontë spirit or to revere the ruins of Wycoller Hall, which many people strongly believe to have been the setting of Fearndean Manor, in *Jane Eyre*.

Wycoller is the sort of place which captures the imagination, and as a result many legends and stories have grown around the place. Ghost stories cling to this small corner of the realm as they cling to few other parts of the north-west of England, and it is not surprising really, when one realizes that this half-hidden, once isolated hamlet has always existed in isolation. Here, on dark nights, terrifying tales of ghostly hounds, waiting in the lanes to seize the unwary, and the spectral horseman galloping down the windswept road, take on real meanings; and the ruined Hall, which has stood lonely and empty for well over a century, will naturally be a fearsome place to the timid who pass this way in the dark.

Wycoller Hall was for many years the home of the Cunliffes of Billington, who were noted personages in their day – the names of successive members of the family are attached to documents relating to the property of the abbots of Whalley. During the Civil War, the loyalty of the Cunliffes to King Charles I cost them dearly, their ancestral estates at Billington were seized, and they returned to Wycoller. About 1820 the last of the Cunliffes died, and the Hall was allowed to decline and become the ruins which are left standing today.

Tradition has it that once each year Wycoller Hall is visited by a spectral horseman, dressed in the costume of the late Tudor or early Stuart period. On the evening of his visit the weather is always wild, with no moon to light the road, and when the howling wind is at its loudest the horseman can be heard galloping up the road at full speed. After crossing the narrow bridge he comes to a sudden halt at the door of the Hall. The rider dismounts and makes his way inside; then dreadful screams are heard which in time turn to moans. The horseman then re-appears at the door, mounts his horse and gallops off in the direction from which he came.

The basis of this haunting is that one of the Cunliffes murdered his wife in an upstairs bedroom, and the spectral horseman is the ghost of the murderer. His victim is said to have predicted the extinction of the family – a prediction which, it seems, has now been fulfilled.

Another version is that the ghost is that of Simon Cunliffe, Squire of Wycoller, who it is said sounds his hunting horn when danger is imminent. This version tells how he was out hunting one day when the fox tried to take refuge in the Hall itself, running up the stairs. Simon, following the creature in hot pursuit, rode up the wide staircase and into his wife's room, causing her to collapse and die of shock.

A more tangible ghost can be found in York Museum, where at 7.40 one Sunday evening in September 1953 a strange thing happened which was to result in a great deal of publicity in the national Press.

On the evening in question George Jonas, the caretaker, was waiting for a meeting to finish and was sitting enjoying a quiet cup of tea. Eventually the meeting closed and, after seeing everyone off the premises, Mr Jonas set out to make a final check of the building before leaving himself. As he left his room, he heard footsteps and, thinking the curator was still in his office, went to speak to him. However, instead of finding the curator, Mr Jonas was confronted by a complete stranger, busily engaged in searching for something in the museum office.

The man was bent over in the far corner of the room. He straightened up as the caretaker walked in, turned round and walked out of the room, passing Mr Jonas as he did so. At first Mr Jonas thought that it was someone who had stayed behind after the meeting, and he followed the man out of the room, remaining a few steps behind him. He later told the Press, 'I noticed then that he was dressed in a frock coat and drainpipe trousers, rather like an old professor, and he wore elastic-sided boots. I noticed this quite distinctly as there were no turn-ups on his trousers.' Mr Jonas then went on to describe how he had followed the figure into the museum library, turning on the lights as he did so, and heard the man speaking slowly, as if to himself, saying, 'I must find it – I must find it!'

The figure moved from bookshelf to bookshelf, rummaging among the volumes, and Mr Jonas went up to him and said, 'If you want to see the curator, I'll escort you across to his house.' As he spoke, he reached out to touch the man's arm, but as he did so, the figure simply vanished, much to his bewilderment. Before vanishing, the man dropped a volume he had withdrawn from the shelf, the title of which was *Antiques and Curiosities of the Church*. The caretaker left the book where it had fallen and the following morning told the whole story to the curator.

Four Sundays later Mr Jonas saw the apparition again. The figure of the old man crossed the hall and simply faded through the locked doors into the library. Again, two or three weeks later, Mr Jonas and a friend heard the turning of pages and saw the identical book drop to the floor. It now became obvious that proper investigations should be carried out to determine just who the phantom reader was, and as a result six people gathered in the museum's library one Sunday evening in December 1953 and sat waiting for the ghostly apparition. A careful check had been made beforehand, and all present, a doctor, a solicitor, Mr Jonas and his brother and two members of the Press, agreed that any form of trickery was out of the question.

On previous occasions the ghost had appeared at exactly 7.40 p.m. but on this occasion it was 7.48 when the first of the phenomena occurred and the gathering heard a rubbing sound and saw a book slowly withdraw from the shelf and drop to the floor, remaining in an upright position. No figure was seen, but the watchers felt their legs become uncomfortably cold up to the knees, and all present were convinced they had been witness to the activity of a supernatural agency.

Theory has it that this was the apparition of Alderman Edward Wooler, a Darlington solicitor and antiquary who had died in 1921 and who had owned the book in question. However, although many people have investigated over the years, since that night in 1953 the ghost has never, to my knowledge, been seen, so it has not been possible for a positive identification to be made. Today one can still experience a feeling of unnatural coldness when researching or reading in the museum library, and it is perhaps only a matter of time before the ghost is witnessed again.

Just outside Eccleshall in Staffordshire is Broughton Hall. Built during the reign of Queen Elizabeth I, it was restored and extended by Thomas Broughton during the reign of King Charles I. Thomas Broughton's initials appear on the left of the

old front door, and in the door itself is a hole, said to be a
bullet-hole. It is said that here one of the Broughton heirs was
assassinated when entering the house, his assassin shooting
him from the branch of a nearby tree. Throughout its history
the Hall has had a chequered life and the story of its haunting
goes back to the time of the Civil War.

We are told that the young heir of Broughton Hall was
standing in the Long Gallery on the first floor when he saw a
group of horsemen approaching. He recognized them as
Roundheads and immediately the zeal of the Royalist youth
was galvanized into activity. Flinging open one of the windows,
the reckless young man shouted down to the horsemen, 'I am
for the King', to which he received a musket bullet in reply.
Although mortally wounded, he managed to drag himself to a
nearby room, where, due to a rapid loss of blood, he
subsequently died. The bloodstains can still be seen today on
the floorboards of the Long Gallery, and no amount of cleaning
over the centuries has been able to eradicate them.

Since that day people have seen the ghost of a young man,
who has been called 'Red Stockings' on account of the red hose
he is seen to be wearing and which he is thought to have been
wearing at the time of his death. The apparition has been seen
standing in the Long Gallery looking out of the window, and on
other occasions he has been seen walking along the Gallery,
before going down the stairs.

About a hundred years ago a young woman from nearby
Charnes Manor was invited to a party at Broughton Hall. A
game of 'hide and seek' was in progress and she went up to the
Long Gallery to hide, creeping behind the door of the first room
on the left. After a few minutes she heard footsteps coming down
the staircase leading from the attics and waited, for what
seemed a long time, for the seeker to find her hiding-place. As
nothing happened, she ventured out into the Long Gallery and
saw a young man, wearing red stockings, looking out of the
window. She took him to be one of the sons of the house, who
wore knickerbockers and thick stockings, and as he had his
back to her, she crept quietly past him and rushed downstairs,
where everyone was sitting down to tea. There, to her astonish-
ment, the son of the house was sitting at the table, so she went
up to him and asked how he had got down before her, as she had
left him in the Long Gallery and he had not passed her on the

stairs. The boy looked at her bewildered and said he had not been in the gallery all day.

Another encounter with 'Red Stockings' is of a much more recent date and concerns a woman from the nearby village who was in domestic service at Broughton Hall. One day, while she was scrubbing the stairs leading from the Long Gallery to the attics, she became aware of a presence, as though someone was nearby, watching her, although as far as she knew she was alone in that part of the house. She looked up and there at the top of the stairs stood a young man. He made no movement, but the look on his face indicated that he wished to come down the stairs, and the woman, thinking that she was in his way, moved her bucket to one side and stood up to let the boy pass.

The figure then began to move down the stairs, but it glided straight towards her, keeping close to the wall and then, to her horror, walked right through her. After that, she absolutely refused to clean the stairs again unless someone was with her.

Is this then the spirit of the long dead heir? From all accounts he was passionately fond of his home, so perhaps his spirit refuses to leave the place, happy to remain within the precincts of this fine building which has so far escaped most modern intrusions.

Let us now go further south and look at the most famous of all London's hauntings.

Elegant Berkeley Square is today as calm and peaceful as any place in the middle of a bustling capital can be. Office workers spend their summer lunchtimes relaxing on its lawns, whilst after dark gamblers and revellers flood into its clubs and casinos, and the traffic speeding through this fashionable district of Mayfair makes it difficult for tourists to hear the nightingale, immortalized in the wartime song. Yet less than a century ago Berkeley Square was the most feared place in Britain.

No. 50 Berkeley Square is today occupied by Maggs Brothers, antiquarian booksellers, and is said to have possessed the deadliest spectral killer of all time, a ghost which caused the deaths of at least two people foolhardy enough to sleep there. No Victorian on a visit to London would have dreamed of going home again without first taking a look at the haunted house in Berkeley Square, and Lord Lyttleton spent a night there, comforted by the company of two blunderbusses loaded with buckshot and silver threepenny pieces, as a protection against evil. He was to report later that during the night he fired at a figure which leapt at him from the darkness and that something fell to the floor 'like a rocket' and then disappeared. Even today no one is really sure of what was the cause or what caused the deaths that alarmed late-Victorian England, for few who saw the killer lived to tell the tale. Those who did generally became incoherent with terror.

The house was the talk of London in the early nineteenth century when Sir Robert Warboys accepted a foolhardy challenge at his club. The handsome adventurer scoffed when friends discussed the possible causes of the disasters at No. 50, and vowed to spend a night there to prove that all the talk of supernatural happenings was 'poppycock'. The owner of the house was a man called Benson. He was reluctant to allow the experiment, but Sir Robert would not be dissuaded, although he did agree, under pressure, to take a gun with him. Mr Benson also insisted that Sir Robert's friends and himself stand guard on the floor below the bedroom where he would spend the night. If anything strange happened, the young aristocrat was to pull the cord which would then ring a bell in the room on the floor below.

Sir Robert retired at 11.15 after a hearty dinner. Just three-quarters of an hour later, the bell began to jangle, and as the rescue party raced upstairs, they heard a shot. They burst into the room to find Sir Robert slumped across the bed, his head dangling over the side. He was dead – but not from a bullet wound. His eyes bulged in terror, his lips were curled hideously above clenched teeth. In short, he had died of fright.

Perhaps the most famous story concerns a curious white-faced man with a gasping mouth whose appearance is said to have terrified two hardened sailors who stumbled one night into the house, which was standing empty at the time. It was 24 December 1887 and the frigate HMS *Penelope* had docked in Portsmouth, her crew heading home for some well-earned Christmas leave.

But two of her crew, Edward Blunden and Robert Martin, arrived in London with little money in their pockets and no lodgings for the night. They wandered the streets for a while before finding themselves in Berkeley Square, where they discovered a 'To Let' sign outside No. 50. There was no doubt the house was empty, and so the two men decided to spend the night there.

They wandered through the neglected rooms, arriving at last in a second-floor bedroom which seemed in better order than the others. Martin was soon asleep, but Blunden was nervous, and as he tossed and turned, he suddenly heard strange footsteps scratching along the corridor outside their room. He woke Martin, and the two shipmates watched, hearts racing, as the door slowly opened and something 'large, dark and shapeless' entered the room.

Blunden anxiously looked around for something he could use as a weapon to defend himself and, as the intruder went after the terrified matelot, Martin seized the chance to escape through the door. He raced down the stairs and ran for help. In nearby Piccadilly he blurted the story to a police officer, and the two hurried back to the house. They were too late. Blunden's shattered body was found impaled on the railings of the basement steps. It appeared as if he had fallen through the second-floor window; his neck was broken and on his face was a grimace of unimaginable terror. The policeman and Martin cautiously searched the house, but there was no sign of the horrible creature that had terrified two tough sailors.

During the 1870s and the early 1880s the occupants of neighbouring houses told of loud cries and moans coming from the locked and empty building at night; the sounds of heavy furniture being moved across bare boards, bells ringing, windows being thrown open and stones, books and other articles being hurled into the street below. At one time the haunted room was said to have been kept locked, and there are stories of a lunatic who died there; others speak of a housemaid who was found lying in the haunted room in convulsions. She died the following day in St George's Hospital, refusing to give an account of what she had seen, because it was 'just too horrible'.

Today the house stands much as it did in the days of gas lamps and hansom cabs. The present firm of Maggs Brothers have held the lease on the property since 1939, and nothing untoward has happened there in recent years, although there are stories told by older residents of the square of a young woman who lived at the house at one time with her lecherous uncle. To escape his attentions she threw herself out of a top-floor window, and her ghost is said to have been seen clinging to the window ledge and screaming. But then, that is another story.

Still in Berkeley Square, No. 53 is reputed to be haunted. During the seventeenth century a middle-aged gentleman lived here with his daughter. After a few years she eloped but, in devotion to her father, promised to return after her marriage. Her father continued to wait for her arrival patiently and more anxiously until he died, more from a broken heart than old age, for his daughter never was to return to her old home.

One moonlit night a few years ago the sad figure of a man, wearing a white satin coat and wig, with lace ruffles at his neck and cuffs, was seen by a neighbour, looking out of the windows on the first floor, overlooking the square. She related later that he seemed to be so sad, with such a hopeless expression. He was seen again one Saturday morning the following year, and over the past few years a number of office workers around the square have reported numerous sightings of him.

Our final London ghost in this section can be found on Gower Street at University College. One of the sights to be seen here is the embalmed body of Jeremy Bentham, the law reformer and natural scientist, whose ghost haunts the main corridor.

Jeremy Bentham bequeathed his body to University College to be used for the purpose of improving the science of anatomy. This was duly done following his death in 1832. Afterwards his skeleton was re-erected, padding was used to stuff out his own clothing and a wax likeness was made by a distinguished French artist and fitted on top of the trunk. 'He' was then seated in the chair which he usually occupied during his lifetime, one hand on his walking-stick, wearing his usual white gloves. Then, with a pack of cards and a £5 note in his pocket, he was enclosed in a mahogany case and deposited at University College, where he can still be seen – at the time of writing – with his embalmed head resting between his feet.

Tradition has it that the eccentric Bentham was mummified against his specific wish, which accounts for the unexplained noises heard from time to time at the College. He is said to rap on the doors and windows of his glass case with his walking-stick to scare the officials of the College into giving him a proper burial.

The case can be found in the cloisters near the main entrance, and one evening quite recently a mathematics master at the University College School heard the tap-tap-tapping of Bentham's walking-stick in the nearby corridor. Thinking it was a practical joker, he walked to the open door of his room and peered into the corridor. To his amazement he saw the ghost of Jeremy Bentham, complete with white gloves and walking-stick! The apparition walked right up to the master and, on nearing him, made a sudden lunge forward, seeming to throw himself bodily at the now frightened man – yet there was no sensation of impact; it was as if he had passed right through him!

On other occasions the sound of flapping wings and the removal of books in one particular lecture room have been attributed to Bentham's ghost, and the sound of footsteps and the tap-tap-tap of his walking-stick are heard so often that they are mainly ignored by most people.

Claydon House at Middle Claydon, near Aylesbury in Buckinghamshire, standing in its own delightful parkland, was built in 1768. It is reported to have several ghosts, but the one which people claim to have seen most often is, strangely, that of a man who died 120 years before the house was built, Sir Edmund Verney, the King's Standard Bearer at the Battle of Edgehill in 1642. He is reputed to walk the house looking for his hand, thought to be buried in the family vault.

When Sir Edmund was captured by the Roundheads at Edgehill, they demanded that he give up the colours. He refused, saying, 'My life is my own, but my Standard is my King's', so he was killed. When the Roundheads tried to remove the Standard from his hand, his death-grip was so like that of a vice that they could not undo his grasp, so they hacked off his hand, complete with its signet ring. We are told that later in the battle the Standard was re-captured by the Royalists, and Sir Edmund's hand still held it in its vice-like grip. Following the battle, his body was buried where it was found but his hand was returned to his family for interment, and the ring was removed and is still in the possession of the Verney family.

In 1923 a forester's wife living on the estate told of hearing heavy footsteps in a corridor when she was looking after the house in the absence of the family. She knew there was no one else in the house at the time and listened nervously as the footsteps stopped at the entrance to a priest's hide. When she went to investigate, there was no one in sight.

The estate carpenter, assisting in the demolition of the large ballroom some years ago, had been working amongst the debris when he happened to look up and see a strange man in unusual clothing standing nearby, looking sadly at the ruined ballroom. When the carpenter called out to the man, whom he knew had no right to be there, the figure simply vanished, although there was nowhere in the area where he could have hidden. It is thought that this was the same apparition that many other people have sighted at Claydon House over the years.

One of the earliest documented sightings was in 1892, when Miss Ruth Verney, then aged about thirteen years, said that she had run up what are known as the Red Stairs and onto the first landing, when, taking a few steps in the direction of the Cedar Room, she caught sight of a man coming down from the upper floor. At first she thought nothing of it, but once she got to the door of the Cedar Room, she suddenly thought to herself, 'Who is he?' and ran back to have another look. The figure had gone. There had been no time for him to get off the corridor, and yet it was empty. The young girl described the man as tall and slender, wearing a long black cloak beneath which she could see the tip of his sword. He carried a black hat which had a white feather curled around the crown in true Cavalier fashion. Unfortunately the young lady does not say whether he had only one hand or not.

Over the years other people have seen ghosts and heard unaccountable noises. One man sleeping in the Rose Room was once awakened just in time to see a dark figure, which quickly vanished into what was later discovered to be a priest's hide. If this is the ghost of Sir Edmund Verney, perhaps one day he will recover his lost hand and then allow his wandering spirit to find eternal rest.

*

Thanks to the publicity-minded Duke of Bedford, Woburn Abbey, standing on the A50 road about six miles from Leighton Buzzard in Bedfordshire, is probably one of the best-known stately homes in Great Britain. Many a tourist to this part of the country includes Woburn Abbey in their itinerary, for with its large collection of wild animals, famous art treasures ranging from furniture and silverware to oil paintings, fourteen state apartments, a few thousand acres of parkland and the odd ghost or two, practically every interest is catered for.

Woburn Abbey, for many years the seat of the dukes of Bedford, was built in 1744 on the site of a Cistercian abbey and is today one of the most popular of the stately homes which are open to the public, but the fact that some 25,000 visitors a week pass through the portals during the tourist season seems to have no affect on the ghosts whatsoever.

One persistent problem, which has happened hundreds of times over the years, was the unexplained door-opening. Time after time the door of the television room would open, followed by another at the opposite end of the room, as if someone had walked through and left the doors open. New locks were fitted; the doors were kept locked, but they still continued to open by themselves, so that in the end the wing of the house was re-constructed, turning it into bedrooms, and where the doors used to be there is now a passage.

The door-opening sessions have now moved and the communicating doors of the Green Bedroom and the Rose Bedroom are now similarly affected. Other incidents occur in these bedrooms too, the most common being what seems like a cold, wet hand passing over the face of the sleeping occupants, and guests who do not know of the presence of a ghost in the rooms are usually quite perturbed after the first night.

The 'unseen inhabitant' is thought to be a young man who was partially strangled, then thrown unconscious from the window, dragged through the park and finally drowned in one of the lakes. Just what he had done to deserve such treatment, or why he should have such a fascination for bedroom doors, one cannot imagine.

When the old abbey was seized under King Henry VIII's programme of Dissolution, the last Abbot of Woburn spoke out against the King's marriage to Anne Boleyn. For this indiscretion he was hanged from one of the oak trees which can still be seen at the south front of the house. It is thought that this could be the cause of the apparition which is often seen in the crypt by visitors, workmen and cleaning staff, who have described it as 'a figure wearing a brown habit'. Apparently this ghost was seen by a host of witnesses in March 1971, during a special club dinner in the beautiful Sculpture Gallery. He was seen standing between the entrance pillars with his back to the room. Then he just floated out through the door.

A chef who lived over the room also saw the Sculpture Gallery ghost, and apparently two ladies who went through the wrong door found him peering at them, wearing a long brown cloak and an enormous hat. Other guests have reported an icy blast around the time when the ghostly monk makes his appearance. One explanation offered for this ghost is that considerable repair work has been carried out in recent years, and possibly this has caused the condition.

Another recent haunting has taken place in the Antique Centre. A female member of the staff was working late in the Centre over the courtyard one night when she noticed the lights were on downstairs, although she particularly remembered switching them off. She went down and was astonished to see a tall gentleman, wearing a top hat, walking around the market stalls. The following day another employee was working late and when he had finished he went upstairs to ask about the mysterious gentleman in a top hat and antique clothes, who had been seen in the market. This particular ghost is unknown, although he has been witnessed quite often, once by a painter who had no prior knowledge of the ghost and also by several foreign tourists browsing round the centre.

Testwood House in Millbrook Road at Totton, a suburb of Southampton, is now known as 'Rumasa' and is owned by Messrs Williams & Humbert, wine and sherry shippers. Although it appears at first glance to be a Georgian building, the façade in fact covers what was once a hunting lodge for King Henry VIII. Since those days it has had a variety of uses, being in turn a nobleman's country seat, a gentleman's private house, a country club and now offices. It is the site of a murder which was committed some 200 years ago, and one would have expected the victim – a young woman murdered by a coachman – to haunt the place. But on the contrary it is the apparition of her killer which has been seen many times over the years.

Heavy footsteps have been heard walking along thick-carpeted passages, sounding as if walking on bare boards, and unexplained figures have been seen outside the house. Two teenagers returning from a dance one autumn evening saw a tall man apparently trying to open the door. As they approached, they called out to him, and the man simply vanished as if into thin air. Shortly afterwards the same figure was seen by a cook, working late in the kitchen. He became aware of someone silently watching him, but when he turned to see who it was, the figure abruptly disappeared. As he drove away from the house an hour or so later, the cook saw in his car headlights the figure of a man in the driveway, walking towards the front door. He noticed the figure wore a top hat, long overcoat and short cape. About three weeks later, another member of the staff saw the same figure standing by the gateway to the drive in broad daylight.

A year or so later the caretaker and his son heard their dog barking late one night. Thinking there were intruders in the grounds, they ran across the yard to the main building, where they found a door rattling violently, although no one was to be seen. After checking doors and windows, the caretaker's son reached the oldest part of the house. Here was a window which was unglazed but covered with a mesh screen and metal bars. As the torchlight fell on the window, the youngster saw the face of a young man staring back at him. The face, long and pale, with grey eyes, looked out unblinking and unmoving as the boy watched terrified. When his father joined him a minute or so later, the face faded away. An immediate search of the building revealed no one inside, and the padlocks were still secured.

A more recent sighting was one evening in February 1972, when the company secretary, having worked late, came down the stairs into what was then the reception room in the main hall and saw what he described as 'a tall dark cloaked figure, which was wearing a top hat, standing near the reception desk'. He said he went 'hot and cold' and hurried past the spectre, which did not move, out through the front door to his car, where, whilst recovering from his ordeal, he made a quick sketch of the phantom coachman.

The manor house at Sandford Orcas stands on the B3145 road, near Sherborne in Dorset. Advertised as 'the Most haunted Manor in the County', this fine Tudor manor house was built about 1540, although there are claims that it is built on the site of an eleventh-century manor.

Open to the public, Sandford Orcas is the family home of the Claridge family and, although reports of ghosts have been made here over a long period, they became aware of strange happenings in the house only in 1966, when their daughter attempted to spend the night in the nursery wing. She left and ran screaming to her own room in the early hours of the morning, claiming that, although she had seen nothing, she had heard loud knocks on the door of the room and had also heard weird dragging sounds.

The house is said to be haunted by the figure of a farmer who, in the eighteenth century, hanged himself from a trapdoor which has long since been boarded up. Mrs Claridge says that she has seen him several times, a white-smocked figure which flits past the kitchen window, usually in mid-afternoon.

The former footman and housekeeper were said to have been afraid to go upstairs alone at night, claiming that the stone carvings of apes above the porch appeared to laugh at them in the moonlight. One lady, a Mrs Gates of Taunton, spent a night in a chilly bedroom off the nursery wing and claims she saw the ghost at the foot of the bed. The figure was outlined against the bedroom window and appeared to be swaying. She said he was dressed in an evening suit, and his face appeared evil-looking. After what seemed a lengthy period, the figure suddenly disappeared.

Other disturbances in the house include mysterious harpsichord music coming from an empty room; a curious haze of blue smoke, which appears in certain rooms; unexplained voices are heard from the inner courtyard or rear wing, and footsteps pace deserted corridors. There is also a photograph in the house taken by Mrs Claridge of members of the family in the garden which also shows a strange unidentified figure which appears to be wearing a white smock.

Several years ago a number of my colleagues from BBC Television went to Sandford Orcas to do a feature on the house. One of the production team said he saw the figure of a man repeatedly passing the kitchen window. He said the figure appeared to be wearing a white milking-smock and an old-fashioned type of farmer's hat. Looking into the history of the house later, he discovered that this was the room in which the farmer had committed suicide – and at the time he was found hanging, he was in fact wearing a white milking-smock.

Mention of television brings to mind Puttenden Manor, just off the A22 road near Lingfield in Surrey. This medieval manor house has featured in numerous television films, commercials and documentaries, and for the camera-toting tourist it is probably one of the most photogenic properties in the whole of Surrey.

When the present owners purchased the property in 1966, the aim was to renovate the old building completely and not only to open it to the public but, living in it as they did, to provide visitors with a view of practically every aspect of English family life. This has certainly been achieved, and the warmth and welcome given by the family to visitors to the house are without parallel.

Puttenden Manor was built about 1475, in the reign of King Edward IV, by Reginald Sondes, as a 'hall house'. Eventually the Sondeses received a title, and Sir George Sondes became Earl of Feversham in 1676. The story goes that the younger of the two sons by Sir George's first wife was insanely jealous of his older brother, and in a fit of rage he killed the heir to the title. In remembrance, his mother planted two weeping ash trees which can still be seen at the rear approach to the house. Legend says that, as long as these intertwined trees stand, Puttenden will be a happy place.

However, insofar as the Sondes family were concerned, the murder of the heir brought about a change in the family's luck and the male line died out. The so-called 'Curse of the Sondes' affected Puttenden's next owners, the Watsons, in the same way, and the titles of the earls of Malton and the marquesses of Rockingham became extinct. In fact, every male heir for the next 150 years died in tragic circumstances.

In 1901 the Honourable Mark Napier bought Puttenden and began the huge task of restoration, which has been effectively continued by the present owners. Present feeling for the house seems to have overpowered the evil, and the general friendly atmosphere has been improved.

When restoration was being carried out, some of the workmen who were employed for the specialist work slept in the master bedroom and complained of having disturbed nights due to mysterious heavy footsteps waking them up regularly. This bedroom was Mrs Napier's original room, but it is the smell of pipe tobacco which is most often experienced here. The present owner says that, although he has not seen the ghost of the previous owner, he is convinced the old man still comes back to Puttenden to sit in his favourite chair and smoke a reflective pipe in peace.

A broadcasting station would, one might think, be the last place where one might meet a ghost. Not so, for amongst the modern sophisticated equipment of the non-stop world of radio and television, something or somebody often lingers, and Broadcasting House, in the very heart of London has not escaped the attention of ghostly visitors. To my knowledge the last sighting of this phantom was in 1937, although he may well have been glimpsed on occasions since. The ghost is that of a tall, bewhiskered butler, carrying an empty tray through the upper corridors. He appears to walk with a slight limp and to have a large hole in one of his socks.

In 1937 at least half a dozen people swore they saw the figure over a period of a few weeks. An engineer found him in a control room on the eighth floor, shrugging him off at first, believing him to be either a musician or a waiter, and went about his work in a different part of the control room. It was some minutes before he realized that Broadcasting House did not have any waiters, and he went to challenge him, only to discover that the strange figure had vanished.

No more was thought about it until later in the week, when

the engineer overheard two BBC producers talking about the mysterious butler and his habit of walking at a sedate pace, holding his empty tray in front of him as though it was laden. He was nearly always seen at a distance of about eighteen to twenty feet and always vanished near a certain door. Another favourite haunt of his was the fourth floor. Three people, one of whom was a newsreader, are credited with having seen him, although only from the back. No one saw his face at any time. No one can throw any light on who the butler was or why he should haunt Broadcasting House, but he is considered important enough to linger into legend.

But perhaps the best-known and most authenticated ghost connected with Broadcasting House is the one regularly seen across the street at the old Langham Hotel, which has become an administrative overspill block for the BBC. Once this was a plush, sophisticated meeting-place for Victorian society, where King Edward VII is said to have entertained Lillie Langtry. Today one could very easily walk past the place and not even notice it – yet one previous gentleman guest persists in staying on, despite the change of ownership and the comings and goings of BBC personnel, and despite the fact that he is no longer a welcome guest.

According to a team from the BBC Radio series *Woman's Hour* who investigated the ghost some time ago, this is thought to be the shade of a Germany army officer who committed suicide by jumping from a fourth-floor window some time before the First World War, after being discovered in an uncompromising position with the wife of a well-known society figure. Those who claim to have seen him describe the figure as thick-set, with a squat head and short haircut and wearing a high-buttoned grey tunic of the Kaiser's army. 'He looks', I was told, 'a bit like an Erich von Stroheim characterization of a German officer in some old Hollywood movie.'

Yet others who have seen him describe him as an elegantly dressed gentleman, not particularly Germanic or military looking but more like a Victorian gentleman in evening dress, with a cloak and wearing a silk cravat in which his tie-pin can clearly be seen. He does not appear to be a creature of habit and has been seen and felt at different times and in various parts of the building. However, several important sightings have occurred in room 333, one of a few guest-rooms used by announcers and newsreaders when working late or early shifts. Two people have seen the ghost quite clearly and for lengthy periods. They are Ray Moore, one-time compère on Radio 2's early morning programme, who saw him in 1971, and newsreader and announcer James Alexander Gordon.

Various people, from producers to commissionaires, have also described encountering the phantom, their descriptions tallying almost identically. All recall seeing the grey cloak, although the facial description alters considerably. The figure appears to be floating well above the floor level; this is borne out by the fact that, because of severe German bomb damage during the Blitz of the 1940s, many of the Langham's floors had to be replaced, and in several parts of the building the new floors are a foot or more lower than the original ones had been.

There are also two areas on the fifth floor which are constantly unnaturally cold – ice-cold in fact, and one man who had worked at the old Langham for a number of years told me that on occasion it was like walking into a deep-freeze, although there was no logical explanation for the sudden changes in temperature.

The ancient town of St Albans in Hertfordshire is named after a Roman soldier who was converted to Christianity and was martyred in the year 303 – the first Christian martyr in Britain. St Albans has many ghosts going back over several centuries, through the Wars of the Roses, in which one of the fiercest encounters was fought here, to the Dissolution of the Monasteries during the reign of King Henry VIII and the English Civil War.

During the Civil War nearby Salisbury Hall was used by King Charles I as a headquarters and armoury; in 1668 King Charles II found other uses for it, secretly purchasing it for his orange-selling paramour Nell Gwynne, and it was here that Nell, concerned for the future of her bastard son by Charles II, after he had refused him a title, held the child out of a window and threatened to drop him into the moat until Charles called out, 'Pray, madam, spare the Duke of St Albans!' Nell's ghost was seen on the staircase and in the panelled hall by George Cornwallis-West, Winston Churchill's stepfather.

The Edwardian era saw a revival of the great days at Salisbury Hall, for when George Cornwallis-West married Lady Randolph Churchill they bought the property and here entertained the society of the day – the Australian opera singer Dame Nellie Melba, the Italian actress Eleonora Druse and even, on one or two occasions, King Edward VII himself. Young Winston Churchill visited the place regularly to see his mother and step-father, writing some of his early speeches in the gardens of the Hall.

But it is the haunted bedrooms which concern us. Often the unmistakable sound of heavy footsteps has been heard in the passage outside the bedroom door. This passage leads to a bathroom, but it once led to the Tudor wing of the house, which was destroyed at the beginning of the nineteenth century.

The great locomotive designer Sir Nigel Gresley – he who designed and built the *Flying Scotsman* – lived here for a few years prior to World War II. When his daughter re-visited the Hall after Sir Nigel's death, she told the occupants that during their stay they were always troubled by strange footsteps in the night. It seems that they later found reference in an old book on the house to a Cavalier who had died unpleasantly at the Hall and whose ghost, complete with a sword sticking right through him, used to be seen frequently.

Another bedroom, a small room over the entrance hall, is also said to be haunted, and over the years children have been disturbed during the night by someone standing beside their beds on several occasions. A governess, spending a night in the same room, said she saw something terrifying come out of the wall near the fireplace and stand beside her bed. Needless to say, she refused to spend another night there.

Secret rooms, priests' hides, stories of suicides and alleged sightings of ghostly Cavaliers and of the ghost of Nell Gwynne make Salisbury Hall a fascinating place. With its labyrinth of secret passages, sliding walls and hidden rooms, even on the brightest of summer days the old Hall seems to cast strange, lengthy shadows, which give it a chilling air.

Hertfordshire is also where we find the last ghost in this chapter, found not in a gloomy old manor house or eerie castle but in, of all places, a bank. The National Westminster Bank in the High

Street, Stevenage, was formerly the Old Castle Inn, and the premises have rather grisly associations.

About 250 years ago Henry Trigg, a local grocer, was leaving the Black Swan nearby when he saw a group of body-snatchers at work in the local graveyard. He was so alarmed at the thought of his own body being stolen that he made an amendment to his will, requesting that his coffin should be lined with lead and placed in the loft of his home. Henry Trigg died in 1724.

About 1850 Trigg's former home was converted into the Old Castle Inn, and when the new proprietor carried out an inspection of the premises he found the coffin still in its original place amongst the rafters. A bit of a nosey-parker by nature, the man cautiously opened it up and discovered the body, well preserved and still with hair on the skull. Alas, Henry Trigg was not to be allowed to rest in peace.

During World War I some drunken soldiers broke open the coffin and took away Henry's bones as souvenirs. They were also used, apparently, to supplement their pay, as most of the bones were subsequently sold to American GIs, anxious to obtain souvenirs of their visit to Britain. Demand far exceeded supply, and so the wily squaddies called on the local butcher to assist.

In May 1970 a workman on the site was astounded to see the apparition of a man, about five feet eight inches in height and wearing a striped apron, glide from the bank into an adjoining barn and vanish on reaching a solid brick wall. Visitors to the area and bank staff have also seen a similar figure with alarming regularity. It has to be assumed, therefore, that this is most probably the ghost of poor old Henry Trigg, perhaps trying to discover the whereabouts of his mortal remains.

4. Ghosts in the Gallery

To my mind, there are few places more exciting – or more eerie – than an empty theatre. The audience may have long since returned to their respective homes, and the artistes retired to some nearby four-ale bar to celebrate a successful opening – or drown their sorrows, following a monumental flop – but the theatre remains awake, alive with the spirits of successes and failures from the past.

Given the opportunity, sit quietly in an empty auditorium, lit only by the working lights, and listen to the breathing spirit of the theatre. Catch its heartbeat in the rustle of a curtain; feel its breath blowing gently along deserted corridors; hear its spirit move quietly amongst the creaking scenery; watch its eyeless balconies and gaping boxes gaze down at you, as they seemingly echo to the distant laughter and applause of long dead audiences, re-living the triumph and despair of long-dead stars.

Many of our theatre ghosts are far more tragic than any drama which might have been played out nightly beneath the proscenium arch. In many theatres it would be ill-advised to tempt the ever-present spirits to put in an appearance, for some actors, it seems, will not 'kindly leave the stage'.

The New Tyne Theatre, in Westgate Road, Newcastle-on-Tyne, is a most interesting theatre and opera house, which was saved from demolition by a dedicated bunch of workers, led by Mr Jack Dixon. It is a Victorian palace of entertainment, full of atmosphere and with a great many stories to tell.

Like many self-respecting Victorian theatres, the New Tyne Theatre also has a ghost, the shade of Bob Crowther, a stage-hand who has haunted the place for nearly a century, after being killed by – of all things – a cannon ball, whilst working in the theatre in the 1880s. Ever since his death, many actors, staff and patrons have experienced a strange and chilling presence on several occasions, and the shadowy figure of a man has been seen walking about the area backstage.

Several years ago a producer was faced with a strike, unless he did something about this ghost which terrified some members of his cast. Faced with such a possibility, he sought the advice of a medium, who told him to try to put the spirit at rest by making it feel welcome and allotting it a certain seat.

So, to make sure that nobody else sits in the allotted seat, a shrouded dummy can always be found in the place reserved for the ghost of Bob Crowther. And where is the allotted seat? In the gods, where else? According to the theatre historian Geoff Mellor, Bob Crowther's ghost is often sighted there, watching events intently. He told me that, when the New Tyne ran as a cinema, the staff became quite used to seeing the figure sitting in the disused gallery and watching 'girlie films'. When the cinema closed for re-furbishing and transforming back into a theatre, someone was heard to remark, 'I bet he's missing Mary Millington!' Since the theatre re-opened with live shows, he has been seen several times, still sitting in his old seat in the gods. When staff have rushed to investigate, nothing has ever been found.

Another much-loved theatre in the North-East which is reputed to be haunted, is the Sunderland Empire, whose foundation stone was laid by Vesta Tilley on 29 September 1906. It says a great deal for the builders of those days that a mere nine months later Vesta Tilley was back to top the bill on the new theatre's opening night. The Empire is haunted by two ghosts and also has a story attached to it, surrounding the mysterious disappearance of an assistant stage manager.

During the early 1950s, while the Empire was playing Novello's *The Dancing Years*, Molly Moxelle, an assistant stage manager with the show, walked out from her digs, leaving all her belongings behind, and has never been heard of since. She simply disappeared. At the time there were a number of rumours but nothing has been discovered to this day as to the whereabouts of Molly Moxelle. Her disappearance is still as mysterious today as it was over thirty years ago.

Mrs Kitty Naylor was a dress-circle barmaid at the Empire for nearly forty years, and she often reported, in later years, having heard footsteps coming down the stairs to the bar. These mysterious footsteps would be heard crossing the front of the bar and appear to return up the stairs. It seems that these footsteps may have been those of the invisible shade of a former assistant manageress who died whilst in the service of the theatre and who used to follow this route each evening to check that everything was in order.

But the best-known and most authenticated ghost is the one which is seen most often in the dressing-room area of the theatre and which is thought to be that of a Mrs Johnstone, a former violinist in the theatre orchestra. Her husband was the theatre musical director, and when his wife collapsed in the orchestra pit, it was he who carried her to a dressing-room, where she was found to have died. Mr Ron Jameson, who in the late 1970s was the manager at the theatre, stated that he saw a lady in a long dress walking up the side of the dress circle, where she suddenly disappeared. Her dress was of the type worn by Mrs Johnstone.

Music Hall was unique. Northerners claim that Music Hall was born in the Star Music Hall, a singing-room attached to the Millstone Inn at Bolton. The Southerners will argue that it was born in 1849 at the old Canterbury Arms at Lambeth in London. However, all will agree that the most famous music hall standing today is the City Palace of Varieties in the Headrow, Leeds.

The City Varieties, as it is now known, has had a chequered career. Like many music halls, it began life as the singing-room of a public house, and it opened in something like its present form on 7 June 1865.

Beneath the theatre there are several passages which are said to extend for miles, even as far as Kirkstall Abbey, some three miles away. Mystery surrounds the coat-of-arms over the proscenium arch which, local legend says, was bestowed on the theatre by King Edward VII, who is reputed to have come incognito to see Lillie Langtry in 1898, when she appeared with Bransby Williams. Edward, as Prince of Wales, was staying as a guest at Harewood House and by tradition he is said to have used Box D, to the right of the stage.

The City Varieties boasts at least two ghosts, to my knowledge. One is that of a female, thought to have been a singer, and the other is that of an old-time piano-player.

One man who has had first-hand experience of the female ghost is television producer Len Marten. He told me, 'It was during the time I was working for Thames Television as associate producer for the television series *Opportunity Knocks*. We were in Leeds doing the yearly round of auditions for the programme. One evening I took my production assistant to the City Varieties Theatre, as she had heard so much about it but had never actually visited the place. At the time there was a revue playing there, and as the manager knew me, we were invited to the circle bar for a drink.

'Several of my contempories were there and we chatted until the bar closed and I went to the cloakroom, which was in the bar area. I had only been in there a moment or two when the lights went out. It was exceptionally dark and it took me a while to grope my way to the door and into the bar. Having got into the bar, I discovered the lights were out in there also.'

Mr Marten could hear his friends chatting as they descended the stairs to the exit and he managed to grope his way to the door, only to discover that it was locked. No one heard him shouting. 'The outcome was that I was locked in the bar for the night, or at least until the night-watchman made his rounds. Unfortunately for me, he didn't.'

So there he was, locked in for the night in complete darkness, except for the glow of a coal fire burning in the bar. Sitting beside it, he gradually became drowsy as the fire died and decided to lie down on a long seat, where he eventually dropped off to sleep. Mr Marten continued, 'I have no idea what the time was, but I suddenly woke up. The room had become ice-cold and as I looked round, I saw, standing by the fireplace, the ghostly figure of a crinolined lady who was looking directly at me. I must have uttered a cry of sorts, as she faded away, seemingly through the fireplace. I saw her as plainly as if she was real flesh and blood. When she faded away, the room became warm again!' I understand that it was not until the early hours of the morning that the night-watchmen eventually came round and let him out.

The Grand Theatre at Lancaster is thought to be haunted by
the ghost of the seventeenth-century actress Sarah Siddons. A
theatre watchman saw her several years ago; she has been
seen in recent years watching a rehearsal in progress, and
more recently the television actress Pat Phoenix, affectionately remembered as *Coronation Street*'s 'Elsie Tanner', told
me that she too saw the ghost, although she could not say for
sure that it was the ghost of Sarah Siddons.

Miss Phoenix told me, 'I was sitting, following a
performance one evening, near the second row of the back
stalls. The theatre lights were out, and only the working lights
were on. I think an electrician or someone was working
backstage. From the exit, there was a break between the stalls
and the back stalls, and it was here that the apparition
appeared. She crossed my vision and, when she reached the
bottom of the aisle, I saw she had no feet.' Miss Phoenix did
not realize until after the figure had disappeared that she had
in fact seen a ghost. She said, 'When one works in the theatre,
one is never surprised at anything. At first I thought it was a
real person. I wasn't the least afraid, nor cold or anything else.
I only realized what it was after she had gone.'

Over the years, other members of staff and touring
theatricals have seen her, although to my knowledge she has
not been seen for a few years now. No one knows why Sarah
Siddons, if that is who she was, haunts the theatre, for she
never actually played there because it was built after her
death. However, the Grand Theatre is built within the shell of
the old Athenaeum, which previously stood on the site for
nearly 200 years, and she had family connections with the
theatre owner.

When I asked Ronald Magill, better known perhaps as the
irascible Amos Brearly in Yorkshire Television's *Emmerdale
Farm*, whether in his long theatrical career he had ever seen a
theatre ghost, he replied that he had had no supernatural
experiences, apart from odd feelings, when working in old
theatres late at night. 'One can almost sense the presence of all
the people that have worked there in the past,' he said. Psychic

investigators have always held that the supernatural phenomena are not apparent to everyone. In other words, whilst one man may see or hear a ghost, another may, like Mr Magill, just sense an atmosphere, whilst a third might be quite unaware of anything abnormal. This certainly applies to the Theatre Royal and Opera House at Northampton, home of the Northampton Repertory Company.

Anyone who has stood inside the stage door in the gloom of a winter's afternoon will agree that, if there is a more eerie corner in Northampton, it has yet to be discovered. This eeriness is not without cause, for this is where, over the years, the theatre ghost has been seen to walk – along the passageway, over the doorstep, which incidentally is an old gravestone, into the carpenter's shop and back again. This is where the apparition was seen one grey December day in 1957 by the late Mr T. Osborne Robinson, who was at that time scenic designer for the company.

He said he was upstairs in the paintshop when he heard footsteps below. He went downstairs to discover what appeared to be a little, shabbily dressed old lady, moving along the passage towards the carpenter's shop. He called out, 'Can I help you?' thinking she was looking for someone. There was no reply. She just walked back and brushed silently past him, her face too dim to be recalled, and disappeared out into the wintry half-light of Swan Street.

Not long afterwards, on Christmas Eve, he was again working alone when the eeriness of the atmosphere became so overwhelming that Mr Robinson, thoroughly frightened, 'downed tools' and fled the building. His assistant at that time was a Mr John Lane, who also had an uncanny experience round about the same time of the year. He was on his own late one afternoon when he suddenly got the unmistakable feeling that someone was watching him. When he looked round into the shadows, he could see no one. Yet the feeling would not go away and was so strong that he got up and switched on all the lights, just to re-assure himself.

A former sceptic who admitted that he used to take the tales of the ghost with just a 'pinch of salt' was Mr Brian Douglas, stage carpenter and theatre photographer. One evening during the summer of 1958 he was talking to someone at the foot of the stairs to the dressing-rooms when he heard footsteps above him. He looked up to see what he called 'the tail end of a woman' in a long, grey-blue garment crossing the passage from his workshop. Like Mr Robinson, he thought she had come in through the stage door to look for someone. He ran upstairs, but he could find no trace of her anywhere. She was not in the passage, the carpenter's shop or the electrician's room. Nor was she outside in Swan Street. She had simply disappeared into thin air. 'Yet', said Mr Douglas, 'she couldn't have reached the door before I got to the bend in the stairs, where I could see her pass.' A sceptic no longer, Mr Douglas realized that what had happened defied logic. He concluded, 'I know there was somebody there – and yet there was no one.'

In July 1960 the little old lady was seen by a painter employed at the time by a contractor re-decorating the theatre. The man was painting on a platform high above the stage when he happened to glance up at the gallery – and there she was, an old lady standing about the fourth step up, wearing what appeared to be a grey costume with some sort of grey jumper, with white stripes on it. She was of medium height, slim and wearing black shoes. She stood looking at him with her arms folded.

He said later, 'I didn't see her face or head, because the ceiling was in the way, with me being so high up. I thought she was just an ordinary person watching the work going on. Then I glanced away for a second, glanced back again and she had gone!' Again there was no time for her to have gone up the steps and out by the ordinary way. She simply disappeared. None of the other workmen saw anything of the old lady, and she did not remain for more than about a minute.

Chief electrician Patrick George described how, when he was in the theatre alone at night, he saw not one but two people in the opposite prompt box. The impact of their presence did not strike him for several seconds, but when he looked again, they were gone. So far as I am aware, the last actor to see the little old lady was Mr Godfrey Kenton, who was with the repertory company in its early years. He reported seeing her sitting in the box on the left of the stage.

In August 1960 two members of the Northampton Tape and Ciné Club spent a night in the theatre, with tape-recorders and cameras loaded with infra-red film at the ready. From 10 p.m. to 6 a.m. they were installed opposite the box where the ghost is said to appear, but their vigil was in vain. They failed even to hear a sound from her. As recently as January 1978 two Northampton boys, James Graham and Paul Merrick, were locked inside the theatre one Saturday night, in a sponsored hunt for the ghostly lady. Both were armed with cameras, but they reported seeing nothing. However, James was to say later, 'We both felt we were being watched by unseen eyes. This was particularly so in the carpenter's shop.'

Who is the little old lady in grey? She seems to be friendly enough by all accounts. There appears to be nothing evil about her. Was she an actress from the past who feels more at home backstage than in the auditorium? No. From my own enquiries, she appears to be the shade of a woman whose home was in Derngate and who leased a part of her garden to allow the carpenter's shop and paint-room to be built. She had insisted on maintaining a right of way, and to do this she had a door put in to open into the shop. It led to four steps, then across the same shop and out of the door in the other side and so into Swan Street. She is probably still maintaining her right of way!

A few yards from the seafront at Margate in Kent, approached from the clocktower, there is a spacious and serene square, a small piece of Margate's gracious past which has survived Hitlers' Luftwaffe and, so far, modern developers. Here in the square stands the Theatre Royal, which, like so many other old theatres, has sadly been converted to bingo.

The Theatre Royal was built in 1787 and is probably one of the country's oldest active theatres. It achieved prominence through two things. its productions and its ghost – two of the latter constantly vying for top billing. Theories abound as to who haunts this old theatre. One wraith is said to be that of an actor who more than a century ago was summarily dismissed. He is said to have bought a seat in a stage box to watch his replacement act out the part which he himself had created, succeeding in bringing the performance to an abrupt and spectacular end by killing himself while he stood on the rail of the box, his body then crashing onto the stage.

Ever after that event, the box had such a weird atmosphere about it that theatre-goers refused to use it. One family who used the box complained that in the gloom they had felt impelled to turn from watching the stage and saw a figure sitting motionless watching them. So frequent were the reports of this apparition that the management were compelled to have the auditorium altered, so that the haunted box no longer exists.

The second phantom of the Theatre Royal is thought to be that of the well-known theatre-lover Sarah Thorne, who died in the 1890s, having set up a good theatrical company and stage school. Two chorus girls are said to have fainted after seeing her figure appear suddenly on stage during a late rehearsal in 1963. In 1972 a painter ran out of the building late one night shaking with fear, after he had encountered her near the stage area.

Sometimes she shows herself as a blob of light, sometimes as small as a golf ball and sometimes pulsating until growing to the size of a balloon, hovering over the stage, in the auditorium and in the dressing-room passages on an erratic journey. During the 1960s this phenomenon was observed by another painter, who refused to continue working in the theatre because of the inexplicable incidents which occurred on most nights. On several nights he had heard footsteps, thumps and a door banging violently and loudly. On one occasion he saw the semi-globular figure, semi-transparent and about ten inches across, glide about five feet from the floor and move from left to right across the stage.

This uneasy, troublesome ghost is regarded as one cause of the misfortune which dogged the theatre until it closed. Some suggested that Sarah, or the long-dead actor, exerted a baleful influence over the place as a revenge for a wrong done to one of them in life. They certainly caused much consternation over the years, bolting emergency doors and unbolting doors securely locked after the public had left, turning out emergency lights and causing the main lighting to come on in the auditorium in the middle of the night. Scenery props have been found to have been moved; lights are still frequently found burning in the toilets, despite having been turned off after the last performance; shuffling and thuds are as common as the lights going on and off, to be followed by a severe icy blast. No wonder a hard-boiled electrician hastily got out of the place and telephoned the police, after he had experienced some of these inexplicable and harrowing incidents.

Another Theatre Royal, this time at Bath in Somerset, is one of the most beautiful theatres in the country, certainly since its restoration. It still retains the original footlights and chandeliers which Sarah Siddons would have known when she played there. As befits such a building, there are said to be several ghosts here, one being rather unusual – a ghostly butterfly, which appears on stage every year during the pantomime season and which has been recorded on film by a local newspaper.

But a ghostly experience of a more sinister kind was encountered by an actor who went into the empty theatre early one evening in 1954 and ran out again within minutes, after meeting the Theatre Royal's best-known ghost, that of a man wrapped in a cape.

The actor walked across the stage to the operating-room stairs, shouting as he did so, 'Hello. Is anybody there?', for the theatre appeared to be empty, despite the fact that the stage door had been left unlocked. Realizing he was alone, he thought it rather strange, not only because the theatre was unlocked but because there were some rather valuable props set out on stage. Suddenly he heard footsteps high up above him. Again he shouted, but there was no reply, save for the hollow ring of footsteps on wood, as if somebody was walking about in the fly gallery, high above the stage.

At first the actor thought someone was having a rather poor practical joke at his expense, by trying to scare him into thinking this was the theatre ghost of which he had heard so much. But he did not believe in ghosts any more than he appreciated practical jokes. Storming off the dimly lit stage, he walked towards the stage door. Just as he reached the steps leading down to it, a very polite voice said, 'Good night, sir!' His blood froze. Having convinced himself the theatre was empty, having heard the eerie footsteps, having experienced the rudeness of the man walking about in the flies who would not even acknowledge him, this polite voice quietly wishing him 'good night' came as the last straw. He was terror-stricken.

Rushing down to the prompt corner and back onto the stage the horrified actor came face to face with the theatre ghost, a man wrapped in a long cape, which at first glance resembled a blanket. He heard the footsteps again as the figure walked towards the auditorium and continued walking – right through a wall. Then a door slammed, far away, high up in the auditorium side of the theatre, causing the terrified actor to run for dear life.

For adding a little spice to a horror film, try joining the phantom movie fan at the Classic Cinema at Lenton Abbey, only a few hundred yards from Nottingham University. This spectre, who has often been seen during the screening of a film, usually makes his appearance in the circle and the projection room. On other occasions he makes his presence known by his footsteps walking down the aisle and by opening and closing doors from the foyer into the main body of the cinema.

According to Mrs Maureen Langford, who in 1973 had been an usherette at the cinema for two years, she had at least one meeting with the ghost. She said she had been for a coffee break and for some reason had looked into the circle. 'I just about dropped my coffee cup when I saw a man just standing there,' she said.

I am told that the cinema is built on the site of Lenton Priory, and for some time there had been talk at the cinema, probably starting as a joke, of the ghost of a monk. But the man Mrs Langford saw was dressed in what appeared to be an ordinary suit. She said, 'He startled me, but because he seemed to be dressed normally, he didn't frighten me.'

On another occasion the ghost was seen in the projection room by Henry Chamberlain, the projectionist. Henry and the manager were the only two people in the building at the time. The manager was downstairs and had just spoken to the projectionist on the intercom, saying he would join him in five or ten minutes. Then Henry looked round and saw a man standing beside him who suddenly disappeared after a few moments, leaving him standing open-mouthed. He said later that there was no doubt in his mind he had seen a ghost and that it seemed friendly towards him. But who he is and why he haunts the cinema still remains a mystery.

The Top Rank Bingo Hall at Sutton, Surrey, was originally one of the many cinemas opened under the Gaumont Cinema's banner in the mid-1930s. Complete with Hammond organ which came up, dazzlingly illuminated, out of the stage, the thousand-seat cinema brought all the glamour and razzamataz of Hollywood into the dreary lives of the people living on the St Helier housing estate nearby. When, during the 1950s, television came within the reach of all, the cinema began to lose its lustre, and the Gaumont was converted into a bingo hall, yet its resident ghost remained as much a mystery as it had always been.

I am told that over the years no fewer than three people are known to have died in this building. A night-watchman was found dead one morning, apparently having suffered a heart attack. Whilst the building was being converted from movies to bingo, a workman was killed and a boilerman died as a result of falling down a flight of stairs. Small wonder, then, that the dim figure of a man in grey has been seen on a number of occasions by the cleaning staff, usually between the hours of six and seven o'clock in the morning.

In the 1950s, just before the conversion to bingo, a number of nearby residents lodged complaints about the sound of the cinema organ being played loudly during the small hours. Much as the manager sympathized with them, there was little he could do about the complaints – for the organ had been taken out several years before!

In 1972 the building was completely re-wired. This meant that the electricians had to work throughout the night. One night one of the men was working on one of the upper floors when he noticed, out of the corner of his eye, the figure of a man standing in a doorway. Thinking it was his mate, he spoke to the figure and, on receiving no reply, turned to face him. To his amazement the figure slowly melted away before his eyes. No one knows who the ghost is, but one interesting fact has been observed; he usually stands a few yards away from the witness and slowly withdraws – unlike most apparitions, he does not suddenly vanish.

Another converted cinema, the Savoy Bingo Hall on Grace Hill at Folkestone in Kent, has a rather interesting ghost. This old cinema stands on the site of a cottage, built about 1870 and demolished some years later to make way for a workshop and yard for a stonemason. In 1918 the 'Electric Theatre' opened on the site, which in 1928 was destroyed by fire and re-built in the 1930s. I am told that during the latter part of World War II a young boy was killed in the re-built cinema, when an extraction fan fell from the roof during repairs to minor bomb damage. By the mid-1960s the cinema had been converted to bingo.

Early in 1972 several members of the staff and some members of the public reported being frightened by the apparition of a woman who often appeared on the stairs, in the staffroom and, on at least one occasion, walking through the closed foyer doors. So concerned were the management at the number of complaints and the number of employees who kept leaving at short notice that they invited a psychic investigator to look into the ghostly goings-on.

Late one night at the end of May 1972, the first of a series of investigations got under way and the researcher reported that, whilst feeling he was being watched by unseen eyes, he walked towards the foyer doors when, to his surprise, a row of seats suddenly snapped down, one after the other.

A couple of nights later the investigator actually saw the phantom lady. He reported that just after midnight the temperature suddenly dropped and he saw, standing near the exit on the opposite side of the hall, the figure of a woman dressed in the fashion of the late 1930s. She was gazing into the centre of the stalls and, whilst doing so, covered her right eye with her left hand, as if brushing away a tear. He dashed towards the balcony for a better view of her, but by the time he had reached it, the figure had gone and the temperature had returned to normal, as quickly as it had dropped.

Again, about a week later, several people stayed overnight in the theatre in an attempt to 'lay' the ghost. Within a few minutes of their arrival, a walking-stick which belonged to one member of the group suddenly raised itself from the back of one of the seats, several rows from where he was sitting. This was followed by the formation of what was described as 'a black, shapeless mass', appearing at one corner of the stage, which then moved along the walls towards the balcony before fading away. The sound of voices could then be heard coming from the balcony, but investigation failed to revealed any cause for the noise. A few minutes later the female phantom appeared about 150 feet from where the group were sitting and was observed to walk through the centre row of seats, before disappearing in the aisle.

Some time later the sister of the boy who was killed was contacted and she produced a photograph of her mother, who had been with the boy at the time of his death. This photograph matched the phantom female who had been seen in the old cinema. When she was asked if her mother had any unusual mannerisms, the investigators were told that she had suffered from a weak eye and so she frequently wiped it – with her left hand!

According to theatre historian Phil Yates, the Theatre Royal at Winchester in Hampshire, began life in 1880 as the Market Hotel. In 1912 the hotel closed down the building and adjacent yard were acquired by James and John Simpkins and converted into a variety and picture house, re-opening on 24 August 1914. About 1916 the Royal, as it was affectionately called, became a full-time revue theatre, but in 1922 the variety acts were dropped in favour of the silver screen, and for the next fifty years it was used solely for the purpose of showing motion pictures, until its closure in 1974. Eventually the theatre was acquired by the Winchester Theatre Fund, and the curtain went up on the re-furbished Theatre Royal on 21 September 1981.

During the Great War, many newcomers destined to achieve stardom appeared here, for it was known in the profession as a 'daisy date' – a try-out theatre for novices who would appear in short melodramas or variety acts, in between the showing of films. Mr Yates told me, 'These acts were known as "lantern coolers", due to the fact that their sole purpose was to fill in whilst the projector cooled down.' At the same time, many famous and well-established acts appeared to give performances in aid of charities. 'These,' said Mr Yates, 'were known in the business as "flying matinées". They would play Winchester in the afternoon, usually to an elite audience who had paid a goodly sum of money, and then they would catch a train back to London in time for the evening show at their own theatre.' Amongst the stars who appeared in such shows were Sir Harry Lauder, George Robey and Dick Henderson senior.

The Theatre Royal houses two ghosts: the shade of the builder and that of a lime-boy. The former, which is seen most often, is thought to be that of John Simpkins. On the cartouche over the proscenium arch are the initials 'J.S.' – according to Mr Yates, John Simpkins wanted to have the initials 'J. & J.S.' engraved up there, and his brother James promised that one day he would arrange for the omission to be rectified. Unfortunately it was never done, and after John died, his ghost was said to return to the theatre periodically, just to see whether James had got around to including the extra initials.

The second ghost, not seen since the years between the wars, was of a lime-boy, who operated the spotlight from the booth at the rear of the upper circle. At the time he was first seen, there was a show running which included an act called 'Eight Dainty Maids'. During one performance, one of the 'Maids' fainted on stage, and on later recovering she claimed to have seen a soldier standing in the wings who reminded her of her dead brother.

Three of the Simpkin brothers staff had in fact been killed in the war, one of whom was the lime-boy. It appears that, whenever a member of staff volunteered for the army, James Simpkins insisted that the entire staff be assembled outside the theatre for a photograph to be taken. One photograph was shown to the girl, who had no difficulty in recognizing the soldier she had seen in the wings. This turned out to be the lime-boy, whose mother had, only the day before the incident, received a telegram informing her that her son had been killed going 'over the top'.

One of the most oft-seen ghosts of the English theatre is that of Sarah Siddons. Perhaps she can be excused for haunting so many old theatres for she was the most famous tragic actress, a great innovator, and she had a passionate love for the theatre. Born into a theatrical family, she conquered Drury Lane in 1782, at her second attempt, staying there for the next twenty-seven years. Her most famous role was that of Lady Macbeth, and her greatest innovation was to depart from tradition by laying down the candle and washing her hands with water from an imaginary ewer.

The dramatist Sheridan Knowles, when asked to describe the effect of her playing, said, 'Well, sir, I swear I smelt blood.' As Katherine in *Henry VIII*, she so terrified the actor playing the Duke of Buckingham's surveyor that he declared he would never again face her before the footlights. Sarah used her power in a constructive way. She was one of the first – if not the first – to discard the powdered wig, hooped skirts and plumed head-dresses that were the mark of the tragic actress of the time. She favoured costumes of simple shape and cleanly draped head-dresses.

It was perhaps fitting that, for her final performance in June 1812, she should choose to play the part she loved most, that of Lady Macbeth. (Although that was the date of her final appearance as an actress, Sarah was still to be seen amongst the theatre-goers of the Georgian era until her death, and as we have already seen, even now, she has not entirely disappeared from the scene.)

The Theatre Royal at Bristol, is probably the oldest theatre in Great Britain, celebrating its 200th anniversary in 1966. From 1778, some twelve years after it opened, Sarah Siddons, following her Drury Lane failure playing opposite David Garrick, played for four very happy years here, before her triumphant return to London in 'The Fatal Marriage' and as Lady Macbeth. Her dressing-room remains at the theatre, and so too does her ghost.

Many actors and staff claim to have seen Mrs Siddons' ghost, which they all think is a benign one. Miss Yvonne Mitchell, whilst appearing in a production of *Macbeth*, was said to have seen a tall, sand-coloured, draped figure standing in the scenery dock. When she looked again, the figure had vanished. Miss Mitchell later said that other members of the cast had assured her she had been witness to the ghost of Sarah, who had herself played Lady Macbeth on the same stage.

Sarah is also resident ghost at the Bristol Old Vic, which she has haunted ever since her lover hanged himself there. One actor who has had experience of her is Frank Barrie, who says that one night he was standing alone on the edge of the stage following a dress rehearsal when he was suddenly tapped on the shoulder. He turned to see Sarah Siddons sitting in one of the boxes at the edge of the stage. Discussing this later with a Shakespearian scholar, the actor was told that she had come to help him, if he had any problems with his career.

Since then Mr Barrie has kept a small poster of Mrs Siddons – given him by his wife – tacked onto his dressing-room mirror. Some time in 1980 he was doing a one man show, *Macready*, based on the actor who was Sarah's protégé. He said that one night he arrived at the theatre feeling ill and tired and wondering whether he could work that night. Although he never touches a drink during a performance, he keeps a couple of bottles in his dressing-room for any guests who might drop by. However, on that particular night, feeling lousy, he reached out for one of the bottles when suddenly Sarah's picture floated down from its place on the mirror. He said he knew then that she was telling him not to have a drink, thus adding to her collection another grateful male admirer.

5. Screaming Skulls

There are a great many bizarre stories to be found in the ghost-lore of Old England concerning human skulls which with a grisly nostalgia refuse to leave the place of their residence and which have been known to make the most hideous screams, whenever attempts are made to remove them. In most cases it is said that the owner of the skull had left instructions as to what should happen to his or her body after death, and if these wishes were ignored, the spirit of the dead person used the skull as a kind of medium in which to carry out the most terrifying hauntings.

For over 200 years the skull of Theophilus Brome has been kept at Higher Chiltern Farm, Chilton Cantelo, near Yeovil in Somerset. Tradition tells us he requested that his head be preserved at the farmhouse when he died, in 1670, and reputed attempts to inter the head have resulted in 'horrid noises' being heard throughout the farmhouse. In the 1860s a sexton began to dig a hole to bury the skull, but when his spade broke in two pieces, he said he would never again attempt an act so evidently repugnant to the quiet of Brome's head.

It is thought that Brome was actively engaged in subterfuge during the English Civil War, and he may have given the directions for the preservation of his head, rather than have some Roundhead cut it from his corpse and stick it on a pike for public exhibition – the fate of some Royalist sympathizers.

During the restoration of Chilton Cantelo church, Brome's tomb was opened and the skeleton was found inside, minus the skull, making it more than likely that the skull which is now preserved in a special cabinet over a door in the hall of the farmhouse is indeed that of the late lamented Theophilus Brome.

A skull at Brougham Hall, near Penrith in Cumbria, is said to have given inhabitants many hours of fear. It was a most formidable and disagreeable relic, for unless it was kept in the hall, the inmates were never allowed to rest because of the diabolical and unearthly screams and noises which continued throughout the night. Whatever they tried to do with the offending skull, whether it was burned or thrown into the river, it had somehow to be restored, so that the spirit of the former owner could rest in peace. In the end, to prevent further trouble, the skull was bricked up into a wall, and it appears to have given no further trouble since.

Similarly, when a new tenant farmer moved into nearby Threlkeld Place, he discovered a skull in a small, dark room which had been kept locked up and unused by his predecessor. The skull was promptly and reverently buried, but the farmer's wife, on going into the room to clean it out shortly after the burial, was horrified to discover the skull grinning at her from the same niche in the wall where it had been first discovered.

Her down-to-earth husband carried the skull all the way to St Bees Head and cast it into the Irish Sea, so one can imagine his horror when, on returning to Threlkeld Place, he found that it had beaten him to it and was sitting grinning eerily in its usual niche. A number of friends came to advise and assist the farmer in his unusual dilemma, but although they made numerous attempts to dispose of the grim find, it always returned by some miraculous means to its niche in the small, dark room. Finally, like the Brougham Hall skull, it too was bricked up in the wall.

Still in Cumbria, one of the most popular folk-tales around Lake Windermere concerns two skulls which could not be destroyed, although several attempts were made. They had been buried in quicklime, cast into the lake and buried in the sides of mountains, yet they would always re-appear. Today it seems the skulls have finally moulded away, but the legend of the Calgarth Skulls lives on.

The skulls were thought to inhabit a small niche on the staircase at Calgarth Hall, on the shores of Lake Windermere, in retribution on the Phillipson family, the owners of the hall. History tells us that Myles Phillipson, a Justice of the Peace, wished to add to his already considerable estate a small tenement owned by an old couple, Kraster and Dorothy Cook, who refused to sell. In order to gain possession of this coveted piece of land and property, Phillipson invited them to a Christmas feast at Calgarth Hall, then, after dinner, he accused the highly respectable couple of stealing a silver cup which he alleged was missing. Somehow the cup was made to turn up on the Cooks' property and, being accused of the theft, they were tried, sentenced to death and hanged at Appleby – but not before Dorothy Cook had laid seven curses on Calgarth, saying that, whilst its walls stood, they would haunt it day and night.

It is recorded that, from that day on, the skulls have repeatedly appeared at Calgarth, defying all attempts to get rid of them. They were thrown out, burned and even ground to powder, but they always returned to the niche in the staircase, until eventually the Phillipson family had them walled up, a solution which seemed to satisfy the skulls, because very soon there were no more Phillipsons left for them to annoy.

Over the years a number of people have gone to great lengths to try to discover the true facts surrounding the Calgarth Skulls. The land and house once occupied by the Cooks has long since disappeared, and a modern dwelling now stands on the site. I have never been able to discover any records of a Myles Phillipson ever having owned or lived at Calgarth, although during the 1650s there was a Justice of the Peace by that name living at the village of Crook. There was also a Christopher Phillipson, also a Justice of the Peace, living at Calgarth Hall who died around 1635.

However, one rather interesting fact does emerge. Up until 1634 the Phillipsons acquired a great deal of land in the area, but after that date the family appear to have suffered and the estates became impoverished by huge fines, the price they paid for their loyalty to the Stuart cause. So perhaps there was, after all, something in the curse uttered by Dorothy Cook, when just before her execution she is reported to have said, 'Hark thee, Myles Phillipson. That tiny lump of land is the dearest ground a Phillipsons has ever bought, for you shall prosper no more – yourself, nor any of your breed. While ever Calgarth's strong walls shall stand, we'll haunt it day and night!'

One of the best-known hauntings surrounding one of these 'screaming skulls' is the ghostly female who haunts the old Hall at Burton Agnes, on the A166 road a few miles from Bridlington on the North Yorkshire coast.

Burton Agnes Hall, the seat of the Boynton family, dates from about 1600 and was built by Sir Henry Griffiths. Old Sir Henry had three daughters, and it is thought that the youngest, Anne, still haunts the Hall today, some 375 years after her death. History records that Anne was attacked by footpads when returning from a visit to the home of the St Quentin family at nearby Harpham. She was so badly injured that she died five days later. At this point historians disagree: some say that the Hall itself was under attack by marauding thieves, that Anne was mortally wounded in the struggle and that, as she lay dying, she asked her sisters to preserve her head at Burton Agnes Hall.

Despite their promises, this wish was not carried out and Anne was buried in the yard of the old Norman church at Burton Agnes. Not long afterwards loud noises, crashes, bangs and moans were heard. Doors slammed and the disturbances became so frantic that the distracted family decided the girl's body should be dis-interred. When the coffin was opened, the head, already a grinning skull, was found to be severed from the shoulders, yet neither the limbs nor trunk showed any sign of putrefaction.

The skull was taken back to the house, and for a time all was quiet, until one day a servant girl threw it out of the window, where it landed on a passing cart. The horse stopped, refusing to move another inch until the offending skull had been taken back into the house. Since then, attempts to bury it in consecrated ground have led to all sorts of trouble. After being kept on a table in the great hall for many years, the skull was finally bricked into a wall, where it remains to this day. But Anne's ghost, known affectionately as 'Awd Nance', is still said to haunt the house she loved so much, apparently inspecting the furniture and making sure the house is kept up to standard.

Collecting skulls was a passion of Dr John Kilner. He had them specially polished and encased in ebony boxes, which he displayed around his home at Bury St Edmunds. But the skull which fascinated him the most was one which he did not own. It was with a skeleton at West Suffolk Hospital where he worked in the 1870s. Part of the attraction was the skeleton's gruesome history, for it was that of a murderer, twenty-three-year-old William Corder, hanged in public at Bury St Edmunds Prison in April 1828, for the notorious Red Barn murder of Maria Marten.

Maria already had an illegitimate child by Corder's elder brother, Thomas, and another by a man called Matthews. (She was the belle of the village of Polstead in Suffolk and was certainly free with her favours.) She had a third illegitimate child to William Corder, which died under mysterious circumstances, and her father pressed Corder into making an honest woman of her. Corder reluctantly agreed, on condition that Maria agreed to go away with him; but in the event she got no farther than the Red Barn, where Corder gave her both barrels of his shot-gun and buried her body under the earthen floor of the barn.

This took place in 1827 and in time Corder was caught, tried and subsequently hanged in public outside the gaol at Bury St Edmunds, on 11 August, 1828. Just as a matter of interest, the whole of the workforce of the town went on strike that morning, in order to attend Corder's execution!

After he had cut down the corpse of William Corder, the hangman secured the remarkable price of a guinea an inch for pieces of the rope from the tumultuous crowd which thronged the scaffold. The rope was said to have acquired certain healing properties after the hanging. The corpse was taken to the Shirehall at Bury St Edmunds for dissection, an astonishing public performance on the part of the authorities of the day. The body was cut open from throat to abdomen, and the flesh folded back to display what was beneath. The remains were laid on a table, and then 5,000 people were admitted to view the gruesome exhibition of human butchery, shuffling past in a gaping, endless stream all day long. At 6 p.m. the room had to be closed in the faces of thousands more hard-stomached wretches still clamouring to see the sight.

Inside the hall, two artists, with the assistance of a young boy who held up the bloodstained corpse, made various deathmasks of the dead man. Those which are still preserved bear only a faint resemblance to William Corder, for the judicial hanging, as carried out early in the nineteenth century, not only stretched the neck but (because hanging was, in those days, nothing less than slow strangulation) also distorted the features. Next day Corder's body was taken to the West Suffolk General Hospital and completely dissected for the learning and information of the medical students there – who at least had some legitimate interest in the proceedings. Corder's skeleton was kept at the hospital and is still used for the teaching of anatomy today. It is complete, with the significant exception of the skull.

Several surgeons got busy on the grisly remains. Part of the scalp was dried and preserved, and this still exists. A book which gives a detailed account of the trial was bound in Corder's skin and can be found in the Moyse's Hall Museum at Bury St Edmunds. The spirit of Corder might not have been too much disturbed at his body being used in this matter, but it is what happened to the skull that was to bring about the haunting.

The skull was stolen from the skeleton in the hospital by Dr Kilner, who substituted a spare one for it. It was then taken to the doctor's home, polished and mounted in an ebony box. From then on there was to be no peace in the house, for, as we have seen, skulls seem to have an extraordinary power to create mischief and disturbance. (This is considered to be because the seat of the mind and thoughts is of great importance to the spirit which has left it.) Corder's ghost, it appears, was considerably angered at Dr Kilner's action and set about haunting him in a most nerve-racking manner. Candles blew out, doors slammed, a strange man in old-fashioned clothes mysteriously appeared and just as mysteriously disappeared.

The doctor soon found the haunting rather more than he could bear, even though he had not, until this point, believed in ghosts. Everywhere he went he heard footsteps behind him and heavy breathing over his shoulder. At night the doors of the house were opened and slammed violently, and his terrified household heard frantic hammering and sounds of sobbing, seemingly coming from the drawing-room where the ebony box containing the skull was kept. Despite his disbelief in ghosts, Dr Kilner knew very well by this time that his theft of Corder's skull was the cause of all the trouble which was holding his household in a grip of terror. It looked as if he would have to get rid of the thing, although it was out of the question to return it to its proper place in the hospital. It was so highly polished that it looked almost tortoiseshell, quite different from the rest of Corder's skeleton. Too many questions were bound to be asked.

In vain he hoped that Corder's disturbed ghost would settle down. One night he was wakened by a noise and went onto the landing with a candle, just in time to see the door to the drawing-room being opened by a ghostly white hand. At that moment Kilner was stunned by a loud explosion, like the report from a gun. He ran downstairs and into the drawing-room, where he was met by a gust of ice-cold air. The box which had contained the skull was lying in small fragments on the floor, and the skull, itself undamaged, was grinning at him from one of the shelves of the cabinet.

It goes without saying that after this incident the doctor lost no time in getting rid of his ill-acquired trophy. He gave it to a friend, Mr C.F. Hopkins, a retired official of the Prison Commission who had bought the old Bury St Edmunds Prison where Corder had been hanged and was living in the governor's house. Rather reluctantly, the retired prison official accepted the unwelcome gift and set off home with it wrapped in a silk handkerchief. On the way home he tripped and fell, and the skull rolled away, grinning evilly, in front of a passing woman, who fell into a dead faint on the spot.

But this was only the beginning of many disasters for Hopkins. Illness, family troubles and financial misfortunes quickly overtook him. He did the wisest thing and took the unwanted relic to a country graveyard, where he bribed the gravedigger to give it a Christian burial. Thus Corder's skull got its ardently desired peace, and we are told that afterwards both Dr Kilner and Mr Hopkins flourished.

The Screaming Skull of Bettiscombe Manor, near Lyme

Regis in Dorset, looks harmless enough, nestling in a cardboard box. It is old and pitted, with the lower jaw missing, and has a yellowing dome, yet it has a frightening reputation which is known only too well in this corner of the realm. Legend says that if anyone takes it out of the house, it screams like a banshee, crops fail and cattle perish. Even worse, the person who removes it dies within the year. The skull's one desire, it seems, is to stay at home in the manor house, and the very last thing it appears to want is a decent Christian burial.

Some years ago a well-known psychic investigator was invited to spend the night at Bettiscombe Manor. He did not sleep well. His room was isolated and the grandfather clock outside his door kept groaning like an ancient pair of bellows. From time to time there was a slithering noise, as if someone in carpet slippers was creeping along the corridor. At exactly 2 a.m. the door creaked open and the investigator forced himself to get out of bed and close it, but thirty minutes later it swung open again and the pitch-black corridor seemed to merge into the room. Suddenly he was wide awake. A yellow light floated in the shadows of the doorway and, even as he watched, it slowly swelled to about the size of a human head. Then, suddenly and horrifyingly, it shaped itself into a grinning skull gleaming with unearthly radiance, its eye-sockets pools of blackness.

Had the skull been warning him not to interfere? It certainly has a nasty habit of getting its own way. A number of years ago a tenant threw it into a duckpond opposite the manor – and a few days later spent hours raking the pond until he found it again, for he had been disturbed by noises of all kinds during its absence and was only too glad to have it back inside again. On another occasion the skull was buried under nine feet of earth, yet it worked its way back to the surface accompanied by frightful screams and deafening thunderclaps. A similar thing happened when a rather sceptical squire stowed it away in a haystack: the skull screamed so loudly that farmers working in the fields for miles around could hear it. And in 1914, at the outbreak of the war, the skull was actually seen to have been sweating blood!

For a good many years the skull was thought to have been that of a Negro slave brought to Bettiscombe from the West

Indies by Azariah Pinney in the seventeenth century, most probably to act as a servant at the house. A Negro servant was something of a status symbol at that time. On his deathbed the Negro uttered a curse that his spirit would haunt the manor until his body was returned to his homeland for burial. No one heeded his prophetic words, and he was quietly buried in the local churchyard. Immediately, the disturbances started. Wild screams came from the tomb, and a poltergeist seemed to have taken over the manor. Bumps and crashes, cries and moans made the night hideous. After a few weeks the body was disinterred and kept in the loft. The spirit appeared to accept the compromise – just so long as the remains were not moved again. Eventually only the skull was left.

Twentieth-century science rather spoilt the story however, when Professor Gilbert Causey, of the Royal College of Surgeons, examined the skull and pronounced it to belong to a prehistoric woman in her early twenties. She may have been some kind of 'foundation sacrifice', slaughtered and buried nearly 2,000 years ago under the foundations of a previous building, which stood on or near the spot, to bring prosperity.

Whatever the truth, the skull has kept a hold on people's imagination for centuries, and it is never allowed out of Bettiscombe Manor these days – just in case!

'Dickie', the resident skull at lonely Tunstead Farm, at Tunstead Milton, near Chapel-en-le-Frith in the Peak District of Derbyshire, is another determined soul. Local suggestion is that it is the skull of a man called Ned Dixon or Dickson, whilst others assert it is the skull of a woman. At all events, it is believed that, should the now incomplete skull be removed from the house, disasters and difficulties will issue until it is brought back.

'Dickie' even succeeded in altering the course of a railway line. Every time the navvies dug the soil of Tunstead Farm, to make the railway link between Buxton and Stockport, the earth caved in on them. In the end, the engineers of the old London & North Western Railway Company surrendered and diverted the track, blaming the 'unstable nature of the ground'. The local inhabitants knew better, of course, and 'Dickie' achieved recognition when a bridge on railway property was named 'Dickie's Bridge'.

'Dickie' was more of a guardian than a curse. When a burglar broke into Tunstead Farm one night, the skull caused such a commotion of thuds and crashes that he was caught red-handed. If an animal fell ill in the fields, 'Dickie' would knock up the farmer by three taps on his bedroom window. But he loses his friendly aspect in a flash if he is moved out of the farm. Then a voice is heard in the wind, with strange moanings coming through the keyholes of every door in the house, saying, 'Fetch poor Dickie back. Fetch poor Dickie back!' He is not very partial to strangers either. He would complain with wails and bangs if he heard what he thought to be intruders approaching the farm, which made him unpopular when itinerant labourers were sleeping in the barns during haytime. On one occasion a couple of these men were so scared by the skull's grumblings that they ran off to the village.

A trio of Irishmen were affected with insomnia caused by the clashing of hay rakes and pitchforks and the honing of scythes in the loft where they were trying to sleep. If they stumbled across, cursing, to see what was going on, the sounds stopped, only to start again as soon as they turned away. Once someone stole the skull and took it to Disley, in the next county. The screamings and thumpings which broke out simultaneously at both Tunstead *and* Disley were so intolerable that 'Dickie' was spirited back, as it were, post-haste!

Much rumour surrounds the identity of the skull. Local legend says that it is the mortal remains of Ned Dickson, who went as a soldier to the French Huguenot Wars of the sixteenth century. A rumour filtered back to England that he had died of wounds, and his wife and cousin took over Tunstead Farm as their own. He was not exactly welcomed back with open arms when he did at last stagger home. In fact, he was never seen again.

But, as with the skull at Bettiscombe Manor, it is more than likely that this too is the skull of a woman, who was murdered at the farm and declared in her final breath that her bones should remain there forever. This is borne out by the frequent sightings of a ghostly female in the house for at least two centuries.

Late one night in the 1860s, Mr Lomas, who farmed Tunstead at the time, was sitting in the kitchen watching over his baby daughter, who lay seriously ill in her cradle. Flickering shadows from the fire licked the whitewashed walls, and all was very quiet but for the gasping breathing of the feverish child. The farmer heard someone come down the stairs and saw a woman's figure slip between him and the fireplace and bend low over the cradle. In the dim light, he thought it was one of the servants and told her not to disturb the baby. As soon as he spoke, the figure vanished – and the baby died minutes later.

Still in the Peak District, at Flagg Hall, about ten miles south-east of Tunstead Milton, there used to be a skull which, despite its anonymity, was celebrated in the neighbourhood and preserved in a glass case. Yet again, horrid screams and moans attended any attempt to dislodge it from its home. Even when they went so far as to arrange a full funeral ceremony, it thwarted all the pomp with supernatural ease.

Before the procession reached Chilmorton church, the black-plumed horses which drew the hearse suddenly shied in the road, as if they had been fronted by an invisible wall. The undertaker tried coaxing, he tried using his whip, but the horses sat back in their traces and defied him. Only when he turned their heads back towards Flagg Hall would they move.

The story is that the skull was once the property of a doctor, who had bought it from a body-snatcher. That being the case, it appears rather strange that it should resist being put back where it belonged – in a grave.

Warbleton Priory Farm, near the lovely village of Rushlake Green in Sussex, was blessed with not one but two skulls. The farm is built of stone from an Augustinian friary which stood on the same site, and when one of its massive walls was being knocked down, workmen discovered the two skulls. For some unknown reason, one was thought to have been that of an idiot.

The first skull was buried, but it tunnelled its way up and was found again the next morning on the doorstep, so they put it in a place of honour on the crossbeams of the house. Later it was afforded a much more dignified position on top of a Bible. The second skull was also preserved, and when it turned up in another farmhouse some five or six miles away, the farmer was none too pleased with his unwanted guest and tried to bury it. The whirlwind which then descended on that sleepy Sussex farmyard soon changed his mind, and he returned it to Warbleton Priory Farm. Both skulls clung to their home like limpets, and even the cows dried up at any threat to oust them; bad luck hung about the house like a thunder cloud. One tenant was so impressed by their talismanic properties that he tried to take one of them with him when he moved to a new farm. Screams and knocking rang through the house, and horses reared up in their stalls, snorting as if the Devil himself had just ridden into Warbleton.

A legend grew up around the skulls that they were those of a murderer and his victim, and a bloodstain that could not be scrubbed away always used to be shown in an upper room. Sometimes, when the moon shone full and low through the trees, people saw a pair of pale, spectral hands fluttering like moths, at a tiny window in the eaves.

In 1905 someone stole the Warbleton Skulls and, rather strangely, all the disturbances stopped at the farmhouse, but who knows what havoc they might have caused elsewhere, since then. And who dared to buy, when one of them was offered for sale in *The Times*, for 10 guineas, in 1963?

The county of Lancashire has a fair crop of screaming skulls also. Browsholme Hall, near Clitheroe in the Ribble Valley, has one, believed to be that of someone who was martyred following the Pilgrimage of Grace, the rebellion which broke out in the northern counties in 1536 in opposition to King Henry VIII's religious changes. When the top storey of the Hall was removed in 1703, the skull was brought down into the family chapel. It was always treated with great respect and reverence, but in the 1850s Edward Parker, then a boy, buried it in the garden as a practical joke. Disaster followed disaster; the façade began to fall away from the Tudor walls; fires broke out under mysterious circumstances, and there were many deaths in the family.

Finally the frightened boy confessed, and the skull was dug

up and returned to its cupboard. Everything returned to normal, but the family had to move out until the house was again made habitable.

At Appley Bridge, near Wigan in Greater Manchester, there stands a rather strange house, known as 'Skull House', riddled with mysterious cupboards, leaded windows decorated with skulls, very low ceilings with thick, skull-cracking beams, boarded-up cellars and various odd nooks and crannies, including a priest's hide.

On a beam in the living-room rests a discoloured human skull which again is said to bring bad luck, unwelcome screams and other disturbances if it is taken out of the house. No one knows who was the original owner of the skull, but it has been at Skull House for as long as people remember, and there are a number of theories surrounding its identity. Some believe it to be the skull of a monk who, whilst being pursued by Cromwell's troops, climbed up the wide chimney to hide in a small room above. Legend has it that the Roundheads, knowing of his attempt to hide, lit a huge fire in the grate, and it was not long before the poor cleric was forced to surrender. It is said that the monk was then beheaded and that it is his skull that rests on the beam, whilst his body is buried elsewhere in the house.

Another theory is that the skull is that of a knight who lived in the days of King Arthur. The story goes that a fierce battle was fought on the banks of the River Douglas and that this skull was found there many years after the event. However, as always, medical evidence adds further intrigue by suggesting that the skull may have belonged to a woman.

Whoever it does belong to, it is determined that the skull should remain in the house, for it is said that ill-fortune will follow anyone who takes it away, and anyway, we are told that even when the skull was once thrown into the river, it somehow managed to find its way back into the house.

Wardley Hall, near Swinton, also in Greater Manchester, has a resident skull preserved in a niche in the wall of the staircase. Over the past two hundred years, some weird tales have been told surrounding this relic.

Tradition tells us that this is the skull of **Roger Downes, the** last male heir of the Downes family, who was an abandoned courtier of King Charles II. While in London on a drunken frolic, he vowed to his companions that he would kill the first person he met and, drawing his sword, staggered along until he met his victim, a poor tailor, whom he ran through with his weapon and killed on the spot. Downes was arrested for the crime, but his link with the royal Court procured him a pardon.

Soon after this, he is alleged to have been involved in a riot on London Bridge, when a watchman struck him with the 'bill' which they all carried, and severed his head from his shoulders. The body was thrown over the parapet into the River Thames, but his head was rescued by his friends and was carefully packed and returned to his sisters at **Wardley.** His sister Maria opened the package and read of her brother's fate from a note which was enclosed.

For many years the bleached skull at the Hall was said to be that of Roger Downes, but round about the year 1780, when the Downes family vault in Wigan church was opened up, a coffin was discovered which had on it an inscription to his memory, and when it was opened, the skeleton was complete with head. Whatever had been the cause of death, the upper part of the skull had been sawn off, a little above the eyes. It was obviously the work of a surgeon, perhaps in an attempt at a post-mortem.

However, to return to the skull. The bone of the lower jaw has become detached, and there are signs of violence to it. Apparently at some time in the past it has been broken up, in an attempt to rid the Hall of the weird happenings.

There is another, more plausible theory attached to the skull, which, like many other skull stories, relates back to the days of Roman Catholic persecution.

The Hall was purchased by the Downes family about 1600, and until 1640 Francis Downes often sheltered his old friend Edward Barlow, a staunch Catholic priest. (Names differ here; some opinion states that it was Ambrose Barlow, a Benedictine monk.) During the Easter of 1640-41 Barlow was seized by a Protestant mob, led by the vicar of **Leigh,** and hauled off to a magistrate at Winwick, about five miles away.

While being held in custody he apparently suffered a stroke, but this did not prevent him from being removed to Lancaster Castle, where he was held for four months, pending his trial and subsequent conviction. At the age of fifty-four he was executed at Lancaster Moor – the site of the present Lancaster Grammar School – surrounded by a large crowd, which included Francis Downes and some of his friends. Downes rescued the priest's head and took it for safe keeping to Wardley Hall.

For a good many years the skull was kept on view at the head of the staircase, and whichever theory is correct, it is a known fact that any attempt to remove it for burial brings repercussions in the form of violent storms and other disturbances. In the past the skull has been burned, cut to pieces and thrown in the river, but it has always, somehow, managed to return to the Hall.

Its real identity is most probably that of Father Barlow, and the story of Roger Downes was possibly put about to hide the identity, at a time when Roman Catholics were hounded unmercifully.

The manor at Turton, just off the Darwen road north of Bolton, is said to have been granted by William the Conqueror to one de Orell, for services rendered during the conquest of 1066. De Orell erected a strong house for defence, which was afterwards known as 'Turton Tower'. It is said that the wages of the workmen were then only one penny a day, but despite this the Tower was built in such magnificence that the family never recovered from financial difficulties.

From the early thirteenth century the Lathoms held the manor, passing it once more to the Orells, descendants of the original builder, in 1420.

By tradition, the Tower is haunted by a lady who can occasionally be heard passing along the corridors and into rooms, sounding as if she is dressed in stiff, rustling silk. The sound is very distinct as she sweeps along the broad, massive oak staircase, which leads from the main hall into the upper rooms. She has also been seen, a lady in black, ascending the stairs leading to the top floor of the Tower and is said to glide across an upstairs room where it seems as if she jumps down an old garderobe shaft, which leads into the original drainage system and which could, in the old days, have been a means of escape, for she no doubt dates back to the persecution and the Orells and is most probably in some way connected with illegal priestly activities.

Recently a wooden cradle was seen being rocked by invisible hands, and there are reports of mysterious bangings, screechings and knockings, which, it is thought, may be connected with the Timberbottom Skulls, now kept in a glass case in the Tower.

A short distance from Turton Tower used to stand a farmhouse by the name of 'Timberbottom' or 'Skull House', so called because of the two skulls which were originally kept there. One appears to be the skull of a female, the other a male, and they were fished out of Bradshaw Brook at Turton around 1751. On examination it will be seen that one of the skulls is badly decayed, and the other seems to have been cut through by a blow from some sharp instrument.

Apparently these two skulls used to rest on the mantelshelf at Timberbottom, and whenever they were removed, all kinds of mysterious activities commenced – bangings, thumpings, screechings and ghostly visitations which drove the tenants near to insanity. They threw the skulls into the river but were forced to recover them because of the disturbances that followed. They are said to have been buried several times at Bradshaw Chapel, but even then they had to be exhumed and taken back. Eventually they found their way to Bradshaw Hall and finally to Turton Tower, where they remain to this day, but by all accounts they still will not remain silent for long.

Who do these skulls belong to? Again we can only look to folklore. In 1882 it was said that they had been obtained by an old woman who claimed that they were the skulls of two robbers, and the following story was told.

Late in the seventeenth century, the family of the house had been away and the house was left in the care of a manservant. One night a gang of mounted robbers came to the house, and one of them tried to gain entrance through a window of the cheese-room. The faithful servant seized hold of a sword and severed the head from the robber. A second member of the gang received the same rough treatment. The headless bodies fell to the ground, where they were picked up by the remaining members of the gang, who made off, leaving a trail of blood and the severed heads behind them.

In due course it was discovered that one of the heads was female, so the story was conveniently changed, and modern versions say that the skulls belong to a farmer and his wife. The farmer is said to have murdered his wife and then committed suicide.

Perhaps the most terrifying story concerning a human skull comes from Staffordshire and Hatherton Hall, which stands about a mile east of Cannock on a lonely part of Cannock Chase. The Hall's isolated position suggests it is suitable for a haunting, and indeed the Hall does have something of a ghostly reputation in the area.

One Christmas Eve towards the end of the last century, a small group of men met at the Hall for the seasonal festivities. Their wives were at a ball, and the men were waiting for their return. Drink flowed rather too freely and in a short time there was none left, so Lord Hatherton ordered his butler to bring some bottles of the best family port from the cellar, where it had been stored for the last twenty years. When the rare and extremely potent vintage was brought in, the men adjourned to the study, where Lord Hatherton showed off some of his trophies – guns, swords, foxes' brushes and stags' heads, which adorned the walls of the well-furnished room.

One of the guests noticed an unusual object on the desk – unusual because it was shaped in the form of a human skull. Picking it up and examining it more closely, he discovered to his horror that it really was a human skull, and he quickly put it back down again. This did not go unnoticed by Lord Hatherton, who walked over to the desk and calmly picked up the skull, holding it up so that all could see it. His Lordship then went on to explain that it had been the head of one of his ancestors, Sir Hugh de Hatherton – but it was now used as a drinking vessel.

Apparently, some years previous the skeleton of old Sir Hugh was dug up, where a private chapel had once stood, and the skull was separated from the rest of the body, cleaned up and lined with silver, and now it was used as a rather macabre drinking cup. Some of his guests considered Lord Hatherton's trophy a little grisly and its use some form of desecration; however, their own wine glasses were re-filled and any fears they might have had were soon forgotten.

After several more glasses of the fine old port, the skull was filled with brandy and passed round so that all present could say they had drunk from the skull of Sir Hugh de Hatherton. They all declared that the brandy drunk from it was the finest they had ever tasted. Such was their merriment by this time that they even drank the health of the long-dead lord of the manor, asking for his presence amongst them so that he too could share in the celebration. Lord Hatherton, more drunk than the rest, said he would surrender the skull should Sir Hugh appear. Little did they realize that their macabre joke was to backfire on them with terrifying results.

At the stroke of midnight the goblet was placed on the desk, and suddenly footsteps were heard in the long corridor which led to the study. Someone suggested that the ladies had returned from the ball, but the sound was that of only one person and the tread was heavy like that of a man. A late guest? All who had been invited had arrived; no guest was missing.

Then, to the stark horror of those in the study, the skull slowly began to move, rolling very slowly across the desk to fall to the floor, where it then appeared to roll under the desk. Suddenly the door of the study was flung open and an icy blast swept through the room. There, in the open doorway, stood the headless form of a knight in armour. The figure remained silent. The guests froze in terror. Then the headless figure bowed and turned, and the sound of his receding footsteps could be heard echoing along the corridor.

It was only the arrival, some fifteen minutes later, of the ladies from the ball which helped to release the tense atmosphere, but every man in the room was now stone cold sober. All of them spent a sleepless night, some afraid to put out the bedroom light.

The following morning an intensive search was made of the study and the remainder of the house, but the skull was nowhere to be found. One of the guests discovered a silver object on the lawn outside the study, and this was found to be the thin silver-plate lining of the skull goblet – but from that day to this there has never been any trace of the skull itself.

Sir Hugh de Hatherton had come to claim what was rightly his, no doubt insulted and thoroughly disgusted by the frivolous use to which the skull had been put.

6. Ghostly Monks

As I drove out to Whalley Abbey, situated in the beautiful Ribble Valley, near Clitheroe in Lancashire, one autumn evening, I could not help wondering what I had let myself in for. I had received an invitation from Ian Green, the manager, to spend a night there and discuss some of the supernatural phenomena that are becoming more frequent in the abbot's house. I was to spend the night alone in the oldest part of the building where most of the activity took place. Although I had not, until that time, heard of any activities in the house itself, I had been told of people who had had experiences of paranormal activity in the abbey ruins.

A middle-aged lady told me how she had been enchanted one evening, as she sat among the ruins, to hear the singing of a Te Deum, which appeared to be coming from the ruined nave. She assured me she was alone at the time. A hard-boiled and cynical reporter from the *Daily Express* told me that both he and his wife had experienced ghostly singing in the grounds, one evening a few years ago. At first they thought it was coming from nearby Whalley church, but on investigation they discovered the church was locked up and in total darkness. Two students told of witnessing a ghostly procession of monks, late one summer's evening. They were astonished to see, coming from the direction of the south transept, a number of monks, heads bowed, hands together as if in prayer, and they watched fascinated for several minutes, until the procession reached the ruined choir and the whole scene faded before their eyes.

Following a television programme I did from the abbey in 1985 in which the present management disclaimed all knowledge of the place being haunted, several people wrote to the BBC claiming to have had some sort of experiences in the grounds, so I was interested to see what the night might bring.

The monks first came to Whalley from Stanlow, Cheshire, in the thirteenth century, after appropriating property which included the rectories of Eccles, Rochdale and Blackburn. In 1289, on the death of its rector, the Pope gave the monks licence to appropriate Whalley church, but it was not until 1296 that Abbot Gregory and a small party of monks arrived to take possession of the rectory house and begin working on the building of the abbey, which was to take over a hundred years to complete.

The last abbot of Whalley was John Paslew, who was charged with treason and executed at Lancaster in 1537, following which the Earl of Sussex was sent on the King's instructions to take possession of the abbey as forfeited property, after the Dissolution of the Monasteries. In 1553 Whalley Abbey was bought by John Braddyll and Richard Assheton, and between them they divided the property. Over the years it was further sub-divided; the abbot's house and infirmary buildings were demolished, and on their site was erected a large dwelling-house which stands today. The ruins and house were bought back by the Church in 1923, and the house is now used as a conference centre, retreat and theological training centre.

All this was on my mind as I drove through the imposing gateway and into the lonely courtyard. As I got out of the car and looked across the darkening and deserted space, I tried to picture Abbot John Paslew as he paced this area many times, deep in thought, before making his decision to light the beacon on Pendle Hill and signal the start of the Pilgrimage of Grace.

Ian Green met me at the door and showed me to my room. We discussed over a drink some of the peculiar things that had happened over the previous twelve months: doors closing by themselves, mysterious footsteps on the stone passage floors, a weird blue light which floats across the grounds, chanting, the figure of a nun who appears periodically in the east wing, and the complaints of visitors who say they have felt someone apparently sitting on their bed during the night.

The room in which I was to spend the night was very cold when I retired, just after midnight. Indeed, the whole of that part of the building was cold, being on ground level and mostly of stone. Having got into bed, I listened to the odd creaks and groans as the house settled down for the night, and somewhere deep in the bowels of the building a door slammed shut quite violently.

Finally I fell asleep, but at about 2.45 in the morning I awoke with a start, roused by what seemed to be a knock on my door. Investigation showed nothing but an empty passage. Then, as I started to return to my room, I heard footsteps – soft footsteps which approached me from the direction of the stairs. These footsteps were certainly real to me, unhurried, steady steps, sounding as if someone was approaching wearing carpet slippers – and they walked straight past me, through a locked door, and faded away along the passage. I can confirm that one's hair really does stand on end under such circumstances.

Apart from my hearing a door slam again later, the rest of the night passed quite uneventfully, much to my relief. My experience was one common to many people who work at the abbey and accepted as a fact of life, although for some reason the present management does not like to discuss them and dismisses them as nonsense. However, I know what I experienced.

A great many of the old houses and halls of Lancashire are haunted by the ghosts of monks and priests. Small wonder, when one considers that the county was one of the last strongholds of the Catholic faith during the period of the Reformation. Many a priest lost his life after being betrayed for celebrating secret Masses. Perhaps one of the best known of these ghostly clerics is to be found a few miles north of Preston, in what is considered one of the top ten haunted houses in England – Chingle Hall, at Goosnargh.

Chingle Hall was built by Adam de Singleton in about 1258, as a small manor house of the cruciform type, surrounded by a moat and complete with drawbridge. It is thought that the timbers used in the building of the house are of Norwegian oak cut from trees which were then over a thousand years old and were retrieved from vessels which had sunk in the nearby River Ribble. Since Adam de Singleton built it, the house has seen many alterations. The cellars, recorded on the original plans, have disappeared, and the drawbridge has been replaced by a little stone bridge. There is now little trace of the moat, except for a small lily pond to the left of the main entrance. The house is riddled with hides and escape routes, the Tudor Singletons being ardent Catholics who, during the Reformation, harboured many priests.

Chingle was inherited by the Wall family, relatives of the Singletons, and in about 1585, despite the persecutions, it became an active Mass-centre. In a tiny signal window still to be seen in the entrance porch, a lighted candle would indicate when a Mass was about to be celebrated, and the faithful would make their way quietly over the fields and slip into the house undetected. In 1620 St John Wall was born here: he was hanged for his faith at Worcester in 1679, and it is believed that his head was brought back to Chingle and buried in the cellars.

There are possibly two spectres at the hall, both monks, one believed to be Franciscan, the other dressed in a black cape and cowl. A few years ago a wooden cross, hidden under several layers of plaster, was discovered in a small domestic chapel, and in January 1977 two cloaked and hooded figures were seen facing the cross as if in prayer.

In 1980 I was asked to investigate the Chingle ghosts for a BBC radio series. I discovered from the occupants that bumps and bangs and other manifestations have made the hall famous throughout Lancashire. Indeed, we recorded footsteps which, as they came nearer to the microphone, turned into a loud buzz. The BBC engineers confirmed that the sound could only have been made by an electro-magnetic force, which perhaps helps explain why our tape-recorders failed to operate in certain parts of the house. We also recorded knocking noises, sounding like a signal, coming from behind one of the many priests' hides.

Other people who have investigated Chingle Hall have taken photographs. One shows a distinct face at a window, in the room over the porch where St John Wall is believed to have been born. One investigator stumbled on an undiscovered priest's hide, after hearing eerie footsteps walk backwards and forwards across the room above the chapel and then disappear into a wall. Expecting to find a body, the investigator and a member of the staff began to knock away the plaster. In the process of doing this, they experienced an incredible phenomenon: they were charged by some invisible being, stamping his feet loudly on the wooden floor. They both turned, expecting to see someone, but the footsteps stopped and they realized that they were the only people in the room. As they turned to continue the work in hand, the footsteps began again and only stopped when they finally broke through and discovered the hiding-place.

In the 'haunted bedroom', the room in which St John Wall is thought to have been born, other phenomena has been experienced. In this room the ghost of a monk has been seen several times, and investigators have experimented with its footsteps, confirming its intelligence. When I heard them, I deliberately stood in the way of their progress, but instead of walking through me as I expected, the invisible being walked around me, and I could feel the floorboards spring as it did so; on another occasion, it moved to one side to avoid me!

Members of the household told of seeing the figure of a monk walk through the gates into the field alongside the hall, but on investigation, when they went outside to look, they found nothing. This same figure has been seen many times by parties of visitors to the house, crossing the bridge and entering the porch, sometimes going up the stairs. Sounds of the dragging of some heavy object have been heard upstairs, along with various rappings and tappings and other noises. These and other phenomena happen at all times of day and night throughout the year, even while parties of visitors are being shown round the house. Articles move as if by invisible hands; pictures have been moved on the walls and flowers shaken in their vases. Objects are quite often mysteriously thrown about the place, and people have been known to feel a friendly hand placed gently on the shoulder. One lady was actually pushed out of the way by this mysterious being, with so much force she was propelled across the room, much to the amazement of the other members of her party.

Perhaps the best-documented phantom monk is the ghost of the Black Canon who haunts Bolton Priory off the A59, about eight miles east of Skipton, on the Harrogate road.

Each years many thousands of tourists visit this lovely ruin, which stands alongside the River Wharfe, in what is considered one of the most beautiful parts of North Yorkshire. The whole area is a scenic delight, and it must have been peaceful in days gone by. However, visit the site after dark, when the moon casts shadows beneath archways and doorways, and even the most hardened and unimaginative will feel a cold shiver run down their spine, for on these occasions it does not need much encouragement for the imagination to run riot.

The Augustinian canons made a start on their priory at Embsay, a few miles away, on land bequeathed to them by Cecily de Romille in about 1120. Round about 1160 the de Romille family provided new lands beside the River Wharfe, and the canons decided this would be a far better site for their church. By moving there, they provided work for many local craftsmen on and off for the next 300 years. Following the Battle of Bannockburn, the priory was plundered by the Scots, and it was not until about 1330 that life was resumed here and a new band of men-at-arms was trained to defend the priory and surrounding lands against all enemies. During the Dissolution of the Monasteries, the brothers were sent packing, but the prior was allowed to stay on and finish his work alone, which is why a small part of the building was allowed to remain intact and become the parish church, still in use today.

Among the many reports from people who have claimed to have seen the ghost at the priory, particularly in the years before the First World War, the eyewitness account of the late Marquis of Hartington remains the most detailed.

In 1912 the Marquis, who was only a small boy at the time, was on holiday from his school at Eton and, with others, was a guest at the rectory during the grouse season. As at Whalley, the rectory is thought to stand on the site of the Abbot's lodgings and the old priory guest-house. One night, on going to his bedroom, the youth was surprised to see a figure standing at the bedroom door. It was a man in his late sixties, dressed in nondescript clothing with a heavily lined and wrinkled face which seemed unusually round and which might have been the face of a woman had it not been for several days' growth of grey stubble on the chin. The boy was at the top of the staircase, looking towards his room at the end of the passage. He ran downstairs for another light, but by the time he had got back to the passage again the figure had vanished.

King George V showed much interest in this ghost and, although he did not see it himself, he heard, with the Duke of Devonshire and Lord Desborough, the Marquis of Hartington's account of what he saw.

In 1913 the Reverend Mr MacNabb, then rector of Bolton, was standing looking out of the window in the rectory when he felt compelled to turn around. On doing so, he saw the apparition watching him from the doorway. It was seen again in 1920 by Lord Cavendish and more recently in 1965, when a man entering the gatehouse saw a figure, dressed in a black cassock with a white overlay of what looked like wool, black cloak and felt black hat, walking towards him. This figure has also been seen by tourists in the ruined choir, in the priory grounds and in the precincts of the church, and the sound of sandalled feet is often heard in the rectory. Most of the more recent sightings have been by visitors in the ruins, in broad daylight, usually in the months of July and August.

The town of Bury St Edmunds in Suffolk is famous as the birthplace of Magna Carta, since there the barons swore to confront King John. It houses the remains of the mighty abbey which once housed the shrine of St Edmund, King of the East Angles, who was murdered by the Danes in 870.

The belfrey of the cathedral church of St James was formerly the ceremonial entrance to the abbey, thought to have been one of the richest in England, and it was partly as a result of this apparent wealth that the abbots were always at odds with the townsfolk. Things came to a head in 1327, when the citizens of Bury rioted and the gateway was destroyed. As punishment, the abbots exercised their powers and ordered the townspeople to build a new gateway, not far from the Norman tower, a task which was completed in 1347.

During the rioting several of the monks were killed, and one is said to haunt the cellars of two buildings in Abbeygate

Street. A local workman reported in 1967 that he had seen a 'grey shape' in the wine vault of a local merchant, and a few months later another man claimed to have seen the apparition of a monk in brown clothes in the cellar of his shop, which was directly opposite that of the wine merchant. It was then discovered that at one time the cellars were joined and connected with the abbey.

But it is the abbey gateway itself that has been most often reported as being haunted. Over a period of years local residents have witnessed the phantom of a monk gliding about the gateway, a place which was once described as 'one of the most spiritually powered spots in England'. Some years ago a local rector claimed to have received spirit messages from several of the abbey monks, who had influenced him when he was writing a book on the life of St Edmund. He claimed that one dead abbot had told him that St Edmund's body had been removed from its tomb and had been buried deep in another part of the church, as a protection against defilement.

Some years ago, as a result of this, an idea was put forward that the site of the transept facing the high altar should be excavated in the hope of discovering St Edmund's remains. However, I am told that the higher church authorities were aghast at the idea and ordered that the ground remain untouched.

Beaulieu Abbey stands a few miles from Brockenhurst at the junction of the B3056/B3054 roads in Hampshire. So many people have seen the phantom monks here, particularly in the area of the Domus Conversorium, that another report of the sighting brings very little response from the staff.

Tradition has it that a group of monks visited King John in 1201 to ask him for exemption from taxation. Their request so angered the King that he imprisoned them overnight, ordering that they be trampled to death by horses the following morning. That night he dreamt that he was flogged for his cruelty, and when he awoke there were whiplash marks on his back. The repentant King released the monks and gave them lands at Beaulieu, together with permission to build the abbey.

Thirty Cistercian monks and an abbot arrived here in 1204 and continued in residence until they surrendered to King

Henry VIII at the Dissolution in 1538. They had worked hard for three centuries at sheepfarming and other agricultural pursuits and during their occupation had created a general atmosphere of wellbeing. In 1209 a certain amount of irritation was caused by the bloodless battle waged by their founder against the Pope, because of his appointment of an archbishop who was not acceptable to the abbey. However, they survived this and also problems associated with the Wars of the Roses and managed to live a relatively peaceful life until King Henry VIII had the monasteries dissolved.

Because of the general peace and tranquillity of the place, it is not really surprising that some of the early inhabitants remain, even though they are mere phantoms. Over recent years the smell of incense has been experienced and footsteps have been heard at night, walking down the grand staircase. In 1928 the ghost of a monk was said to have been seen at Beaulieu by a lady visitor. He told her to dig in a certain spot where she would find a coffer containing two round stones and some bones. She is said to have found them and given them a Christian burial, and since then several visitors to the abbey have reported hearing the devotional chanting of monks in the ruins. In the 1960s another lady visitor in the Domus Conversorium saw the shadowy figure of a monk in a brown habit, seated in a recess near the magnolia, who appeared to be intently reading a scroll of parchment.

Still in Hampshire, crouching low in the Downs just off the A3 road between Petersfield and Horndean, stands the picturesque village of Buriton. The heart of the village is a pond, on one side of which stand the church and rectory and on the other a large and sprawling manor house which, like so many up and down the country, has been added to over the centuries.

There are several ghost stories attached to the village, but the most important ghost of Buriton is that of a friar who has been seen by at least half a dozen people over the past few years. In the 1960s an eleven-year-old boy was living at the manor who was a keen horseman. One Sunday evening he brought his pony into the stable yard and was startled by a man whom he later described as looking like a monk in a dark brown cloak, standing silently behind a bale of straw. It never entered his head that the figure was anything other than human, and his fear was not of the supernatural but of a rather menacing human stranger loitering in the yard.

At first the boy said nothing, but he made an entry in his diary, and his parents noted that he was reluctant to go to the stable the following day. Later in the week his mother noticed the diary, and what she read made her contact the local vicar, who talked to the boy and asked him to show him the spot in the yard. The boy described the man in detail: the brown habit, the white cord fastened round his waist, but he could not describe the feet as they had been hidden behind the bale of straw.

What the boy told him convinced the vicar that what he had seen was not a monk but a friar. Although Buriton had never had any monastic institution, the manor had been owned by the Benedictines before the Reformation and had always been let to a tenant farmer. As the story of the ghostly friar spread about the village, the vicar was told by a member of the church that about a year before the boy's sighting, when she and her daughter had been gathering wild flowers near the spot where a narrow lane from the village crosses the busy A3 road, they had seen a man dressed like a monk in a brown cloak and white cord with tassels and had assumed it was someone trying to frighten them into thinking they had seen a ghost. Angrily the woman approached the figure, which was about a hundred yards away, but as she neared the little monk, he vanished on completely open ground.

This and subsequent reports led the vicar to look at old church records and in particular the notes and records left by his predecessor, a canon who had been incumbent from 1936 to 1952. From the reports, it appeared that the previous vicar had been working in the garden when he noticed a brown-robed figure approaching along the avenue of beech trees behind the house – an area of trees long known as 'Monk's Walk'. He put down his spade to see what the stranger wanted, and almost at once the figure vanished. The canon would not accept a supernatural explanation, but his wife said that she too had been in the garden on many occasions and had heard footsteps from the area of 'Monk's

Walk'. One afternoon they had been so loud and clear that she had assumed her husband was returning home, and she went into the house to put the kettle on for tea.

Over the past few years the little friar has been seen a number of times at these three sites, all within a radius of two miles, along a line of an ancient track leading from Buriton to Winchester. On this track too, some distance beyond the place where the lady and her daughter saw the friar, there is an ancient stile shown on old Ordnance Survey maps as 'Friar's Knapp'.

Unlike the monks of old, the friars did not remain within the precincts of the monastery but wandered from village to village on regular circuits, finding hospitality where they could or sleeping in the open. Perhaps this little friar so loved the countryside around Buriton that his spirit prefers to continue to amble gently through the Downs and villages in this most beautiful part of the country.

Among London's haunted churches, St Dunstan's in East Acton is said to be haunted by monks who are often seen walking – sometimes singly, sometimes in procession – up the centre aisle.

In the 1930s a former curate stoutly maintained that he had seen ghostly monks in the church, and in 1944 the then vicar realized that there was something strange about the place and that ghostly monks did walk there. He reported that on many evenings he had witnessed up to a dozen monks walking up the centre aisle and into the little side chapel. He said they wore golden-brown habits and were hooded, although one of them was a violet-hooded monk, who kept himself apart from the others and with whom the vicar claimed to have had a number of conversations.

On hearing these stories, the Press sent an intrepid reporter along to the church and told him to remain there until he had established once and for all whether or not the monks walked. After a couple of hours sitting pretty bored and waiting for something to happen, the reporter fell asleep, but very soon he was jerked awake and had to pinch himself to make sure he was not dreaming, for there, walking slowly towards him, were six monks in hooded gowns. Standing up to bar their way, the reporter nearly fled in terror when the ghosts passed right through him.

St Dunstan's church was built just over a century ago, and nearby there stood a mansion called Friar's Place. During the Middle Ages a Chapter of St Bartholomew the Great existed on the site of Friar's Place, and in those days it is most probable that monks would have walked in procession – or singly – where the church of St Dunstan's now stands.

St Giles church, near Denmark Hill underground station at Camberwell in south-east London, is only about 150 years old but it is thought to be the fourth or fifth church to stand on this site. Adjoining the church is a small, narrow passage, the 'Churchyard Passage', which leads through the old graveyard to the site of Clergy House, now demolished. Some years ago local residents claimed to have witnessed the figure of a priest walking slowly along the footpath and, although they knew it was a ghost, said they found it far from frightening. It was thought to be the ghost of a friendly old priest who regularly used the passage to return home in years gone by.

In the 1970s two teenagers reported seeing a shadowy figure approaching them in the pathway one evening, and they recounted their experience to the vicar of St Giles, who then made an appeal in the church magazine for any similar incidents to be reported. A number of letters were received from parishioners who claimed to have witnessed the figure of a man in the same locality, although it appears that since the early 1970s the sightings have become less frequent.

Perhaps the best-known haunted church in London is that of St Magnus the Martyr, by London Bridge, where over the years dozens of people have reported seeing an unidentified robed figure in broad daylight. Many visitors have claimed to have sensed an unusual atmosphere as soon as they entered the building.

The church of St Magnus the Martyr was built by Sir Christopher Wren in 1676 on the site of a previous church that had been destroyed in the Great Fire of London of 1666 – a church which had stood on the site long before the Norman Conquest of 1066. Amongst those buried there – in the old church – was Henry de Yevele, master mason to three kings, Edward III, Richard II and Henry IV, and who was one of the architects of Westminster Abbey. He died in 1400.

The church is haunted by a robed figure, thought to be a former priest. A verger once found himself within a couple of feet of the ghost one Sunday afternoon following a service. Everyone had left, the door was locked, the lights were on, and the verger was putting something away in a small cupboard beside the altar when he saw the figure immediately in front of him. The figure was stooping, as if looking for something on the floor. 'Can I be of any assistance?' enquired the verger. At this, the figure straightened up and, smiling, just faded away. He saw the figure on two other occasions, a short, black-haired priest wearing a cassock, who was kneeling before the Blessed Sacrament in the Lady Chapel. Each time he spoke to it, the figure faded away.

One afternoon a church worker was doing some needlework in a modern addition to the church when a priest in a cassock walked into the room. He circled the table in the centre of the room and then disappeared through a wall. Some time later she saw the same figure again, this time in the vestry one Saturday afternoon. She said that, as she worked, she became aware of a figure in a cassock standing by her side. She could see the ribbing of the serge quite clearly, but yet, when she looked up, she could see neither body nor face. Frightened, she walked out of the room without looking back.

The figure was seen at an early Mass one Sunday morning when, as a lady in the congregation turned her head to make her offering to the church collection, her eye caught a movement behind her. Turning round, she saw a priest wearing a cassock walk up the nave and seat himself in the pew behind her. She really took him to be a priest, expecting him to go and put on a surplice and assist with the Mass. When he did not, she turned round again and found he had gone. Later, when she asked the verger about the priest who had come in during the church collection, she was astonished when he replied that no one had come in and no one had occupied the pew behind her.

On another occasion a man working in the church asked who the priest was who did not appear to trust him. He said he kept coming in the church and watching him working, very intent on seeing the work done correctly. A choirboy ran up from the crypt one day, looking very frightened, and said that he had seen a robed figure on the stairs who had disappeared into one of the walls.

General opinion is that this is probably the ghost of Miles Coverdale, the sixteenth-century English translator of the Bible. He was Bishop of Exeter and a friar – and where he was witnessed by the verger apparently looking for something is the exact spot where he is buried.

The Little Abbey Hotel, now a private hospital run by AMI Healthcare, on the A4128 road at Great Missenden in Buckinghamshire is believed to be part of Missenden Abbey, and some think it dates back to the twelfth century. For many years it has been the haunt of a phantom monk.

Apparently an unknown monk is believed to have committed suicide in 1297 for fear of disciplinary action about to be taken against him for dallying with a local married woman whilst her husband was away at the wars. The scandal which resulted from this incident is said to have been the cause of the abbey's being closed down.

Some years ago the Little Abbey Hotel was used as a preparatory school, and it was during this time that a secret tunnel was discovered, which led to the Great Abbey – its entrance, a trapdoor in the ballroom bar, has now been sealed. It is believed the 'Little Abbey' was built for nuns of the same Augustinian order, and this tunnel was used by monks to gain entry into the building to provide – amongst other things – the Sacrament to the nuns.

A number of years ago servants could not be persuaded to enter what is now the lounge, and as recently as 1972 some rather unusual incidents were still taking place. Early one morning the hotel handyman was repairing a window on the top landing when he saw the figure of a man in a brown, hooded cloak coming up the stairs. He had his hands together as if in prayer, and as he passed, the handyman wished him a polite 'good morning' and turned back to his work.

A few moments went by and, as no one came up or down the stairs, the handyman was puzzled as to where the man was going. Other than the toilet, the rooms on this floor belonged to resident members of the staff and were all locked. He checked the doors and the toilet, yet he was unable to find any trace of the figure or explain his disappearance. Staff are quite convinced that this is a little monk, possibly the same one who kept their predecessors away from the lounge.

The village of Checkley stands on the A50 road between Cheadle and Uttoxeter in Staffordshire, and Checkley church and its churchyard have been the scene of some unusual events over the years.

I am told that, when the churchyard was still in use for burials, there was great difficulty in obtaining the services of grave-diggers to work there, not because of a shortage of manpower but because they disliked the atmosphere, always having the feeling of being watched by unseen eyes.

Back in the late 1930s, a Miss Stonehouse was the headmistress at the little church school. One Sunday evening in winter she had a very disturbing and mysterious experience when returning home. No one ever crossed the churchyard after dark, despite the fact that it was a short cut to the school house, but in a hurry to get home on this particular cold and wet evening, Miss Stonehouse decided to go the short way across the churchyard; she had crossed it in daylight hundreds of times and knew every twist and turn. She started out – but was stopped half-way. Fear gripped her and, although she tried desperately to press on, some invisible force held her back. At one point she thought she had come up against a headstone or even a tree, but she could not discern any shape. Still the force held her back and she had to return, thoroughly frightened, to the church and make her way home by the road. The following day she went across the churchyard in daylight but could not find anything – no tree, no headstone, no obstacle in her path.

During her time at Checkley school, Miss Stonehouse had the vicar's permission to practise on the church organ, something she did frequently. When she was finished, it was her habit to go to the church tower to turn off the lights, and then she would have to grope her way back to the door, lock it and leave the key at the rectory. She had never had the slightest fear, the church always felt so friendly, but once or twice she thought she could see a hooded figure near the altar as she stood at the other end of the church. Whatever it was, she was not afraid, thinking perhaps it was a trick of the light through the window.

One day she mentioned it to the vicar and was surprised to learn that he had often seen the figure of a hooded monk slipping into the shadows when he was in the church. He thought it was the ghost of the abbot of Croxden, whose grave was in the chancel, side by side with those of the Foljambes, the usurpers of his abbey.

Lindisfarne – Holy Island – in Northumberland is about ten miles from Berwick-on-Tweed and is reached by crossing a narrow causeway from Beal, just off the A1 road. The priory, Lindisfarne Castle and the whole of the surrounding area from the mainland to the island are steeped in ancient history. The Vikings landed here in 793, and many relics of the period have been uncovered in recent years. The monastery was founded in the seventh century and was destroyed by the Norsemen, led by such terrifying warriors as Ivor the Boneless and Erich Bloodaxe. Following the Norman Conquest of 1066, the early monastery was re-erected as a priory.

The present ruins, dating from Henry VIII's Dissolution of the Monasteries, are now owned by the Department of the Environment, and the castle, built by stones from the priory as protection against the ever-present threat from Scottish raiding parties, is administered by the National Trust. For over 300 years it remained a ruin, until it was renovated and made fit for habitation by Sir Edwin Lutyens, the designer of the Cenotaph in London.

If one stands on the ancient rocks near to the priory ruins, particularly on a bleak, grey day, with the ever-present wind tugging at one's clothing, it is not difficult to visualize the terrified monks, all those centuries ago, rushing across the beach with their relics and valuables, pursued by the bearded Vikings, their battle-axes swinging, swords flashing and their cries of victory following the decapitation of a fleeing monk. In fact, the monks put up a valiant fight for their treasure, and much of it was saved, but at the cost of most of their lives.

It is thought to be the ghost of one of the victims who is seen periodically drifting quickly across the causeway to the security of Beal. Those who have seen him often admit to having no previous knowledge of the history of the area and are usually surprised to learn that the apparition of the grey-clad figure they have clearly seen, often in great detail, could in fact be that of a man killed whilst trying to protect the priory treasures over a thousand years ago. It is only after he has faded into the sand that realization may suddenly dawn.

One of the most amazing stories I have come across which concerns a phantom monk allegedly took place in the vicarage of Elm, a village on the B1101 road, a mile or so south of Wisbech in Cambridgeshire.

The rambling seventeenth-century vicarage is said to be haunted by a brown-clad monk who died over 750 years ago. It is also haunted by a bell that sounds the death-knell, following which the vicar would invariably hear of a death in the parish within twenty-four hours. I'm told that, over a period of $2\frac{1}{2}$ to three years, this occurred no fewer than thirty times.

But it is the ghostly monk which is of most interest. It appears the hauntings began with accounts of unexplained footsteps heard night after night after night. At first the vicar used to get up and investigate, thinking that perhaps there was an intruder in the house, but as he was always unable to locate the footsteps, where they came from and who made them, he decided after a short while to give up trying to locate their origin and wisely remained in bed.

The footsteps continued for some months, and then the vicar's wife brushed against the ghostly monk one evening in an upstairs corridor. She claimed the figure spoke to her, saying, 'Do be careful' and she – with far more pluck than the author – asked him who he was, receiving the reply, 'I am Ignatius the bell-ringer.' He appeared to be wearing a light brown monk's habit and sandals. The vicar's wife claimed that after that first incident she met the monk many times, and gradually he told her his life story, saying that he had died in the twelfth century in a monastery which had originally occupied the site of the vicarage.

The phantom monk allegedly said that one of his responsibilities had been to watch the floodwaters rising in the

Fens and to warn the brothers, presumably by ringing the bell, if there was any danger. One night he fell asleep and did not see the water rising, failing to warn the brothers when it got dangerously high. Subsequently the water rushed into the monastery, some of the monks were drowned and poor Ignatius was disgraced. According to the vicar's wife, he was a man about thirty-three years of age, with dark curly hair and thin features. She said she saw him only at dusk and always wearing the same brown habit and sandals, which were old and worn.

The most remarkable event took place one September, when the vicar's wife slept, as she often did, alone in another room. Her dog invariably slept with her, but on this occasion he whimpered and cried and repeatedly ran out of the room. But when she kept bringing him back, in due course he settled down to sleep on the bed. The vicar's wife then switched out the light and was soon sound asleep.

Suddenly she was awakened with the feeling of being strangled. Terrified, she was then picked up and violently thrown sideways across the bed. Speechless with terror and unable to scream, she became aware of a vague dark shape looming over her, and through a haze a pair of gnarled hands which were clutching at her throat. As the hands tightened their grip, she had to use every ounce of willpower to fight the increasing pressure, being powerless to defend herself physically. Then, from the dark recesses of the room, she saw the figure of the little monk appear. He came towards her and, reaching for the hands clutching at her throat, he pulled them away. As the pressure on her throat relaxed, she dropped back onto the bed, exhausted.

Hardly had she time to catch her breath before she became aware of a vague creature with a huge head and a red face bending over her again. Her dog was snarling and snapping at something invisible. Summoning all her remaining strength, the near-hysterical woman tore herself free and rushed into her husband's bedroom. Her throat was badly bruised and the marks were to remain visible for several days afterwards. The room was locked up and never used again following these terrifying incidents.

When she next saw Ignatius, the little monk explained to

her that she had been attacked by the spirit of a man who had been murdered in that room. He said that, now he had saved her life, he had gone some way towards completing his penance and was hopeful of complete forgiveness and rest.

There are a number of well-authenticated ghost stories attached to the parish church at Farnham in Surrey.

One day a visitor to the area was kneeling in quiet prayer at the back of the empty church when, raising her eyes, she was surprised to see a pre-Reformation High Mass being celebrated at the altar. She told the local newspaper how she had sat spellbound as she had watched the gold-clad priest and his brightly dressed servers, wreathed in what appeared to be incense vapour. The church seemed to have suddenly become half-filled with people, some moving up and down the aisle, others sitting motionless, but unlike the priest and his servers, they were grey and colourless. It was only the arrival of the rector and a churchwarden that shattered the strange atmosphere, and she found the church suddenly empty again.

Apparently, during the Second World War someone reported hearing men's voices chanting in Latin coming from the dark and empty church. They investigated and noticed a number of pin-points of light at the far end of the nave, moving about as if numerous candles were being carried in procession around the interior.

A former vicar is on record as saying that on several occasions, whilst preaching the sermon, he saw a semi-transparent veil descend, cutting off the altar and chancel, and he could make out figures and lights moving dimly behind the veil. Other visitors to the church have witnessed similar phenomena.

Finally, Westminster Abbey in the heart of London stands on a site used for a church or abbey as far back as the eleventh century, and there is some evidence that it was used for religious buildings by the kings of the East Saxons prior to the year 616. Legend has it that in that year St Peter himself appeared to a Thames fisherman and guaranteed large catches of fish on conditon that one tenth would be given to the clergy at Westminster. An abbey was certainly built on the site by

Edward the Confessor, although he did not live long enough to see it completed.

The present building was started in the reign of King Henry III, but it was not until the end of the fifteenth century that the church, as originally conceived, was completed. The Henry VII Chapel was added in the early 1500s, and the west front and the flanking towers were completed in 1734. The abbey has been the accepted place for the coronation of English monarchs since the eleventh century and the site of tombs of many monarchs from the time of Henry III.

During the numerous modifications, the floor level has gradually been lowered by some two feet, which accounts for occasional reports from night visitors and cleaning staff of the ghost of a monk gliding about with the bottom of his habit some distance from the ground. Who he is, no one really knows, but it is possible he could be one of the former inhabitants, probably Father Benedictus. Until recent years he had not been seen since the 1930s, and when he appeared in 1932 his feet were only a matter of a few inches from the floor. But his best performance – if that is what it can be called – was given in 1900, when he was seen clearly as a Benedictine monk, standing with his hands hidden in the sleeves of his habit and with his cowl half covering his head. He walked backwards, looking at the people in the south transept, and after a full twenty-five minutes of haunting he disappeared through a wall. Despite what the abbey staff might tell you, there is absolutely no foundation for the legend that he is the ghost of a monk killed in the abbey.

Whilst visiting Westminster Abbey, you might like to keep a look-out for the ghost of John Bradshaw. He was president of the Court which condemned King Charles I, and he haunts the deanery to expiate his signing of the death warrant. A more tangible ghost is that of a soldier dressed in the uniform of the First World War, wounded and muddy from the Flanders battlefield, standing with head bowed in sorrow a few feet from the tomb of the Unknown Warrior.

Some people believe he is the ghost of the warrior himself, whilst others think he is the brother of the soldier buried there, but no one will ever know. The bodies of four complete unidentified British soldiers, killed in four corners of France during the First World War, were covered with a Union flag and one was chosen by the general in charge to become the Unknown Warrior. The body was brought home on 11 November 1920, given a State Funeral and interred in earth brought from France and covered with a slab of stone quarried in Belgium. A fitting tribute to 'Tommy Atkins'.

7. Phantom Nuns

On a June night in 1956, seven workmen settled down to sleep in makeshift beds and sleeping-bags which had been provided for them on the ground floor of Watton Abbey, on the A163 road near Driffield in North Yorkshire. The owner was selling up after a tenancy of over thirty years, and the workmen had been brought up from Nottingham to help with the three-day sale of the old abbey's furniture and fittings.

A strong June wind howled round the reputedly haunted building as they slept. Then, at about one o'clock in the morning, above the high wind could be heard the eerie tolling of a bell. Every one of the workmen awoke at once and sat bolt upright in their beds, spines tingling and the hair rising at the back of their heads – for they knew that the abbey bell had been removed many years before. One man was so afraid that he dived head first through a window, injuring himself as he landed rather awkwardly in a flowerbed. The auctioner's foreman, in charge of the men, grabbed a shot-gun, loaded it and fired both barrels skywards. This had the desired effect: the bell suddenly ceased its tolling.

As one, the men picked up their beds and bedrolls and spent the remainer of the night in a large marquee which had been erected in the grounds of the abbey to hold the auction. They were taking no chances, for there was no doubt in their minds that the ringing of the phantom bell was the work of Elfrida, the headless ghost of Watton.

According to legend, Elfrida was a beautiful young girl who, on entering Watton Abbey as a novice, was victimized by the abbess, said to have been jealous of her youth and good looks. Unable to bear the harsh penances imposed on her, she ran away and was seduced by the first man she met, who then promptly deserted her. Pregnant and full of remorse, Elfrida returned to Watton and confessed her sins to the abbess, who sentenced her to death.

However, although the ghost is real enough (she has been sighted many times over the years), the story behind her nocturnal wanderings is too fanciful by far. She is unlikely to go back beyond the seventeenth century and, as history records, is more likely to be the ghost of a woman beheaded during the Civil War.

During that time bands of Roundhead troops stormed across the Wolds following the defeat of the King's army at Marston Moor. The owner of Watton Abbey was a staunch Royalist who was fighting for the King many miles away, and his wife, left with only a few servants for protection, took her child and her valuables to a small room from which there was a secret exit from the house. Unfortunately the soldiers found the other end of the exit as they poked around the area of the moat and, rushing up the stone steps, broke down a panel leading to the room. The child was dashed against the wall and killed, her ladyship was struck down and beheaded, and the house was plundered.

It is more than likely that this ghost is that of the unfortunate woman who now haunts the abbey grounds and surrounding area, seeking not a recalcitrant lover but the child so cruelly taken from her by the men of Cromwell's Model Army. She is said to be harmless enough, although quite frightening to encounter, because she has no face, just a black void beneath the cowl of her cloak.

Holy Trinity church in Micklegate, York, was once part of a Benedictine priory attached to the abbey of Marmoutier in France and is said to be haunted by the ghost of its last abbess, a woman and a child.

History records that the abbess defied soldiers sent by King Henry VIII to carry out his policy of Dissolution, saying that they would enter the convent only over her dead body. Obligingly the soldiers killed her. As she lay dying, she promised she would haunt the place until another sacred building rose on the spot, a promise she kept until the convent was demolished completely, when she moved into the church. She is often seen on Trinity Sunday.

There was great excitement one hot August Sunday morning in the late nineteenth century when a worshipper saw three figures, two women and a child, move across the east window. The two women were seen quite clearly against the window itself. One was tall and graceful and the other of average size and build, who appeared to be caressing the child as if to soothe it. No one is certain who these ghosts are, although the tall, graceful figure may well be that of the abbess, and the others the wife and child of a man who is buried near the organ window. Not long after his death, his only child died of the plague and was buried in a great pit, still to be seen outside the city walls, whilst his wife, who also died of the plague shortly afterwards, was buried with him in his grave near the organ window. It is said that the spirit of the mother would not rest without the child and that the spirit of the abbess brings the child from the grave outside the city to the grave of her parents, in Holy Trinity church.

In 1876 a worshipper recorded having seen a light, formed like a female, robed and hooded, glide rapidly from north to south at some distance outside the window. The figure returned some time later, accompanied by that of the child. The child was not seen again, but the woman hurriedly completed the last trip across the window.

In 1981 I made three separate attempts to photograph the inside of Holy Trinity Church. On the first two occasions the film broke inside the camera – something which has never happened to me before – and on the third occasion I exposed a full roll of HP3, using an electronic flash, and not one of the thirty-six exposures came out, yet just after I took several photographs in other parts of York without difficulty.

Still in York, the Theatre Royal in St Leonard's Place opened in 1740 on the site of the old St Leonard's Hospital, founded by King Stephen in the twelfth century. As was the custom in the Middle Ages, it was run by nuns, and the theatre itself is haunted by the ghost of a young nun who is said to have broken her vows and as punishment was walled up alive.

This explanation, which is common in accounts of this type

of haunting, may be a distortion of the true facts. A spokesman for the Roman Catholic Church told me that in the Middle Ages it was a fairly common practice for nuns to show their commitment to the religious life and rejection of worldly goods by having their cell doors bricked up, leaving only a small window through which to receive food and drink.

Whatever the reason behind this haunting, there are several people, including a former Lord Mayor of York, who are prepared to testify that a ghostly nun does tread the boards here, still wearing her grey-and-white habit. She is most often seen in a small room near the dress circle. Many occupants of the room have said that they were aware of a strange feeling, as if they were being watched. Others experienced an inexplicable chilling sensation, and I was told recently that strange things still occur today. Not long ago a well-known actress standing at the back of the dress circle saw the figure of a nun, dressed in grey and with a white coif, leaning over the edge of the stage box.

During the autumn of 1975 whilst rehearsals were in progress for *Dear Octopus*, the cast, assembled on stage to sing 'Kerry Dance Again', were puzzled to see a light slowly develop in the dress circle. As they looked on in fascination, it increased in intensity and eventually took on the head and shoulders of the nun. This little incident lasted for only a few seconds, but it brought the rehearsal to a complete standstill until the cast had recovered their composure.

In 1965 some members of the cast of a current production managed to obtain permission to try to 'lay the ghost'. Several members of the cast and theatre staff occupied the small room near the dress circle, and after a very short period of time they heard footsteps. The atmosphere became cold and eerie and, to their absolute horror, the figure of a tall woman suddenly appeared, hooded and gowned, having entered the room through a closed door. Unfortunately, just at that time a female member of the company began to scream with fright, and the apparition vanished.

A great deal – far too much, in fact – has been written about Borley Rectory. Here was a good haunting which was exploited in the most cynical fashion until it became history's most profitable ghost story. This dark and gloomy mansion on the border between Essex and Suffolk, just off the A134 road north-west of Sudbury, has been described as 'the world's most haunted house', and even though it burned down mysteriously in 1939, its legend lives on in strange happenings near the spot where it once stood.

The twenty-three-roomed Borley Rectory was built in 1863 for the Reverend Henry Dawson Bull. As soon as his family moved into the newly built red-brick house, they began to hear puzzling sounds at night. Footsteps and tappings were heard, followed by the ringing of bells and voices answering, and a ghostly chanting was heard coming from the nearby village church. It was not long before the disturbances took on a more physical form. One of the Bulls' fourteen children was awakened one day by a slap in the face. Another claimed to have seen a figure standing by her bed, and a nun, a phantom coach and horses and a woman in white have all been reported in the grounds by servants and passers-by.

But it is the persistent stories of the ghostly nun which have carried down the years. Some say she is the spirit of a young nun who eloped from nearby Bures convent centuries ago and who, on being caught, was buried alive, while her lover, a monk, was decapitated. But a London medium claimed that she was told the Borley ghost was that of Marie Lairre, a nun induced to leave her convent at Le Havre, France, to marry a member of the Waldegrave family of Borley Manor, which formerly stood on the site of the rectory. She was allegedly strangled by him in May 1667 and buried in the cellars.

The Reverend Mr Bull, far from being put off by his spectral tenant, was fascinated. He did her the honour of building a summerhouse in his garden, opposite the 'Nun's Walk', a long path skirting the lawn, in order to watch her. There are no records of her walking at night, but always during daylight, particularly at dawn and dusk. Henry Bull's son Harry followed the family tradition and was ordained, becoming his father's curate, and the two of them would spend hours sitting in the summerhouse, smoking their pipes and watching for the nun, which they claimed to have seen a number of times.

At dusk on 28 July 1900, as four of the Bulls' daughters were returning to the rectory from a garden party, they were crossing the lawn when they all saw the nun, dressed in black, head bowed, hands clasped in prayer. Miss Ethel Bull saw the nun on numerous occasions, and all the family claimed to have seen other apparitions, including a ghostly coach and four which would come clattering down the narrow lane beside the Rectory, waking the household and bringing white faces and round eyes to many bedroom windows to see the celebrated sight.

In 1930 the Reverend Lionel Foyster and his wife Marianne moved into the rectory, and the baffling incidents continued. Curious messages started appearing on the walls and scraps of paper urging, 'Marianne, get help.' Mrs Foyster also heard disembodied female voices calling her name, and she was later attacked by an invisible assailant. Soon after that the couple fled to a more peaceful home.

Psychic investigator Harry Price, founder of the National Laboratory of Psychical Research, was called in to investigate the rectory and its ghosts. He reported drops in temperature of up to ten degrees, curious incense-like smells, stones and cakes of soap thrown across rooms, and books moving as if of their own accord. A Benedictine monk trying to hold an exorcism in the rectory was hit by flying pebbles.

The next occupant was Captain W.H. Gregson, who re-named the house Borley Priory, but the new name brought no better luck, and in 1939 it was destroyed by a fire which was started mysteriously. Several people claimed that at the height of the blaze they saw a girl at an upstairs window. Witnesses told the village policeman that a grey-clad nun had been seen slipping away from the inferno. In 1943 excavations revealed fragments of a woman's skull and skeleton four feet below ground, together with a number of religious pendants. Still the arguments raged. Some claimed they proved the existence of the hapless Marie Lairre, whilst others insisted they were the remains of a plague victim from earlier times.

The rectory may be long gone, but its supernatural residents have outlasted it. In 1951 a man standing at the end of the Nun's Walk saw the figure of a woman who moved slowly down towards the end of the neglected garden and, on reaching the boundary hedge, vanished. Council houses are now standing on the site of the former garden of the rectory, but stories continue to be published to the phantom nun, still to be seen gliding down the Nun's Walk, usually on 12 or 29 July.

Strange as it may seem, although Lancashire was one of the last strongholds of Catholicism and a great many of its spectres are of priests and monks who suffered for their faith, I can find only one vague reference to a phantom nun, and she is of comparatively modern origin and appears to have died of nothing more dramatic than natural causes. She can be found in a school on North Road in St Helens, which was once a convent attached to Lowe House Roman Catholic church. The nun is quite familiar to recent pupils, and appears in, of all places, an upstairs lavatory which apparently is on the site of an earlier dormitory. No one knows the identity of the ghostly nun, but it has to be assumed she was a member of the order that inhabited the convent who probably loved it so much in life that her spirit now refuses to leave.

A particularly interesting ghost can be found at Heskin Hall, in the village of Eccleston, near Chorley. Although she is not a ghostly nun, surely she deserves a place in this chapter for she was murdered as a result of the actions of a cowardly priest.

Heskin Hall was until quite recently a School of Management under the ownership of the Lancashire County Council, but its weathered gateposts and much of the existing building date back to the reign of Queen Elizabeth I and saw a great deal of activity during the Civil War, when this part of the country was fanatically faithful to the Royalist cause. Like many of the major Lancashire family homes, Heskin Hall was a Catholic household, and the ghostly figure seen from time to time is reputed to be that of a young woman who was hanged by a cowardly priest to save his own skin.

Having been discovered hiding behind a secret panel by Colonel Rigby, one of the Parliamentary commanders for the area, the priest immediately denied his faith. Just to prove he was of the strongest Protestant persuasion, Colonel Rigby demanded that the priest should personally put to death the young Catholic daughter of the house, a girl sixteen years of age. This the priest did, hanging her from a beam, still to be seen at the top of a fire escape. (It is considered lucky to touch this beam nowadays.)

Since that time, the girl's ghost has repeatedly been seen at Heskin Hall, and there are stories of a number of people who have left rather hurriedly, after a midnight visit from the ghost in the Scarlet Bedroom, which many still find extremely cold despite central heating. Others claim to have seen the priest chase the young girl across the room, which is nearest to the crime. Both forms then disappear through the wall close to the location of the beam.

The ghost has also been witnessed – although only vaguely in the now modernized kitchen, and a recent visitor to the Hall, alone at the time, is said to have encountered the ghost so clearly and so solid-looking that he spoke to her thinking she was a member of the household. In fact, no member of staff was on duty that night and the Warden was on holiday.

On my files there are a number of accounts of hauntings by nuns or monks, from various parts of the country, and in most cases they evoke no fear, usually the opposite, a feeling of warmth and comfort which they apparently bring to the places where they have appeared. This is perhaps as it should be, for, after all, they were men and women of God, who had in their earthly days devoted themselves to acts of charity and kindness. Occasionally, though, one does come across people who have been terrified by these gentle ghosts, and one such case comes to mind from London, in which I am honour bound to let the people concerned remain anonymous.

About thirty years ago, in the Wandsworth area of London, there was a severe case of haunting which took place in a block of flats and which so disturbed one tenant that she had to seek psychiatric help. The flats had been converted into a huge and rambling block from an old convent, a maze of corridors and dark places which housed thirty or more families at the time. A number of them related some frightening and disturbing experiences.

One tenant, whom I will call Mrs Smith and who had lived in the flats for over eight years, claimed to have seen the ghost of a nun on several occasions, dressed from head to toe in black. Mrs Smith lived in one of the best flats, large and airy, on the first floor; it was believed to be the old Mother Superior's room. She said that her experiences began almost from the day she and her family had moved in.

On the first occasion they were all sitting in the living-room when a gust of wind blew right through the flat, although all the doors and windows were shut. A few weeks later Mrs Smith's sister came to stay for a few days, and on one occasion she was washing up in the kitchen and talking, as she thought, to Mrs Smith, but Mrs Smith was elsewhere in the flat. She could hear the conversation but was unable to make out what was being said, and she afterwards asked her sister whom she had been speaking to. Her sister replied, 'Why, you, of course; you were standing right behind me!'

There had always been a feeling about the place, that they were being watched by unseen eyes, but this presence was not to remain invisible for much longer. Both women began to catch glimpses of a dark, shadowy figure. It was no definite shape – no hands, no face, no voice, just a rustling dark shape. According to Mrs Smith, the apparition would begin its walk near the large original fireplace in the living-room, glide through the hall and then disappear in the entrance to the bathroom. One day she followed the shadowy figure along what she had now named 'the nun's walk', but when she got as far as the bathroom doorway, the figure completely disappeared.

Her husband was, of course, sceptical about the whole thing. He merely laughed and told her it was just an association of ideas, particularly as they both had known the building when it was in use as a convent. He treated the whole matter as a huge joke until one day something happened which terrified him. He came into the living-room, his face white with fear and terribly shaken. When Mrs Smith asked him what was the matter, he replied in a shaking voice, 'I've just seen your bloody nun!'

In another part of the building, where the old convent chapel once stood, another resident told how she both saw and heard the phantom. She said she was sound asleep but for some unknown reason suddenly woke up aware that something was not right in the flat. It was a feeling she could only describe as 'an overwhelming sense of someone nearby'. Thinking it might be a burglar, she switched on the bedside light, only to discover the room empty. Hurriedly she got out of bed to go to her children's room and make sure they were all right, but she had no sooner got into the passage then she froze in her tracks – for standing right in front of her, no more than three or four feet away, was the dark figure of a nun. She said she could see the face, which was round and pleasant, and she is sure that the nun spoke to her in some way, saying, 'Don't be afraid. Just say, God be with you,' following which the figure then seemed to merge into the gloom of the passage and disappeared. The poor woman was frozen to the spot for several minutes before daring to move, although she later said, 'There was nothing at all evil about it.'

This same tenant owned a modern sideboard which was quite out of keeping with the room and surroundings, and one evening there came from it some rather strange and ominous knockings and tappings. A friend was visiting at the time and the tapping had begun whilst they were sitting chatting over a cup of tea. I was assured that the noises were definitely coming from the inside of one of the cupboards, and when the cupboard door was opened, in an endeavour to find out what was causing it, a gust of ice-cold wind blew across the room. 'It wasn't a draught,' I was told. 'It was a real wind which came from *inside* the sideboard cupboard.' Then both tenant and guest saw the casement window open as if by some unseen hand, and this was followed by something far more frightening: the bedclothes were violently thrown off the bed and piled in a heap at the bedroom door, which led into the living-room and which was open. Just then the children rushed into the living-room crying, obviously very frightened. When they were asked what was wrong, they said they had seen the 'nurse' again. She had been looking at them through a window. (The children had mistaken the habit of the nun for the uniform of a nurse.)

Another family, living in what was known as the chapel wing, said they often heard the soft tread of numerous feet crossing their ceiling, sounding just like a procession of nuns going to prayer, although at that time no one lived upstairs in that part of the block, because it had not then been converted into flats.

Although she has been nicknamed 'the sinister sister', it appears that the phantom nun is not in any way deliberately trying to frighten the people, although one can readily appreciate the alarm she must cause the residents from time to time. At the time of writing, the flats are still standing and, as far as I am aware, they are still occupied.

8. At the Drop of a Glass

Until fairly recent years, the inn, like the church, was a focal point of the community. On winter evenings the locals would gather round the roaring fire telling and re-telling the stories and legends of generations, or listening to the tales told by passing travellers. Perhaps it was the travellers themselves who, as victims of a leg-pull, brought away with them terrifying tales of apparitions which are said to haunt some of our older inns. No doubt some of the ghost stories told over a quiet drink were a mixture of fact and fantasy, but a great many of them were not, as some of these ghosts are still said to rattle their chains from time to time, even today.

A great many of the inns and public houses of old England are reputed to be haunted; just how many are is open to debate, although a great many books have been written covering the subject of haunted inns. This chapter contains some of the better-known ones which the tourist might find to their liking, because, whether you believe in their ghosts or not, these establishments are well worth a visit for the beverages alone.

Let us begin in London and a fashionable public house long said to be haunted by a ghostly soldier. The Grenadier in Wilton Row, not far from Marble Arch, once served as a mess for officers in regiments stationed nearby. The times are recalled by Old Barracks Road, an alley which runs by the pub. It appears that in the old days the main bar was situated in what are now the cellars, and what is today the main bar was then the officers' dining-room.

The story goes that one September many years ago an officer was caught cheating at a game of cards and was immediately handed out some rough justice by his companions. He was flogged on the spot and staggered down to the cellar, where he died. As a result his ghost is said to haunt the pub to this day.

Because the fatal card-game took place in September, it is during that month that the disturbances at the Grenadier are at their worst. One September a young boy lying in bed with the door open saw what he described later as 'a shadow of someone on the landing'. As he watched, the shadow grew larger and then smaller, as if someone had approached the bedroom, then retreated. The following September a woman customer said she distinctly saw a man going up the stairway from the bar, who vanished before he reached the top. Another guest sleeping at the pub found himself suddenly awake in the middle of the night and sensed, rather than saw, someone who appeared to be standing, trying to reach out and touch him, from the foot of the bed. Almost as soon as he became aware of the presence, it disappeared again.

Other peculiar happenings include, from time to time, knocks, raps, lights being switched on during the night, taps turned on, objects being moved and unexplained shadows which move along the landing and staircase, even during the day.

One of the oldest buildings in the Hackney Road is the Nag's Head, which has a ghost in the cellars. It was witnessed by a barman in 1968 when, getting a case of whiskey from the spirit store, he suddenly looked up and saw the figure of an old woman in a grey shawl and long black dress, standing in a corner. A few weeks later the landlord persuaded the barman – who until then had refused to go back down the cellars – to bring up a crate from the store-room. After waiting several minutes, the landlord went into the cellar to find the barman standing frozen and staring at something, which he himself could not see. The old woman had returned again. No one knows who she was – perhaps she was the original Old Nag. Certainly she still makes her presence known by the sound of her footsteps crossing the floor of a disused upstairs room.

Another interesting London pub is the Plough Inn, a

150-year-old pub near Clapham Junction railway station. One of the intriguing aspects of this old place was the existence of a hidden room. From the outside, three windows can be seen on the top floor, and yet the rooms in this area contained only two. In 1970 an entrance was found to the mystery room and the additional window was blocked up – despite which it is still found open from time to time.

The pub ghost is known affectionately as 'Sarah', and although she is known to affect the pub dog, to my knowledge she has been seen only once in recent years. That was round about the time the mystery room was discovered and a resident barman woke during one night to see the figure of a woman with long black hair and wearing a white gown standing in the corner of the room. Other staff claim to have experienced 'cold spots', prickly sensations and the feeling of being watched by unseen eyes.

Sheppeys Restaurant in Shepherd Street in London's Mayfair is perhaps the oldest house in the area, a combination of restaurant and club-bar, which has in its 300-year history been a haven for Royalists, footpads, poets and courtesans. Its first tenants were said to be 'of low standing' because they were connected with the theatre – and, indeed, part of Sheppeys was converted into a theatre, one of the first in London.

During the eighteenth century, to accommodate the needs of cattlemen from the Shepherd Market, the ground floor became a coffee-house, and Boswell, who lived nearby, often brought his friend Dr Johnson in for refreshment. The upper floors then developed into lodgings for young gentlemen and disreputable characters, one of whom was a notorious highwayman, who stored his loot in a tunnel which is said to lead from the cellars to Marble Arch – the old gallows site of Tyburn.

The fancy wrought-iron gate to the vaults was the original front door when Sheppeys was the home of the dandy 'Beau' Brummell, who may have given elegant parties there to which the Prince Regent may have been invited. Indeed, the ghost might well be that of Beau Brummell, for he is said to have had a great sense of fun. On the other hand it might just as well be the ghost of the highwayman – no one can be sure.

Whoever he is, he has been seen scores of times by the cleaners early in the morning, and they also claim to have had their bottoms pinched, to have been moved gently to one side and to have felt him tug their dresses. The figure, when seen, is always described as being tall and thin and dressed in a long black coat. His features, however, are never clearly seen and always seen to be hidden in shadow. It is a pity really, for otherwise he might be more positively identified. Despite efforts to exorcise him over the years, he still haunts the two bars and puts in an appearance from time to time.

247 Baker Street, not far from the fictional site of the most famous apartments in London, is the address of The Volunteer, a popular pub built on what was once agricultural land on which two farms existed. It is haunted by a ghost which has been identified as that of Rupert Nevill. He and his family were Royalist supporters during the Civil War, and he is known to have been involved in the Battle of Naseby. The entire Nevill family were wiped out in 1654, when they died in a fire which swept through one of the farmhouses, and it is for this reason that the pub is haunted.

Perhaps because of its age – it was built in 1794 – the pub would have been suspected of harbouring a ghost, but when considerable alterations were carried out in 1963 suspicion turned to postive fact. Lights would be turned off and on, and footsteps were often heard about the place. Then an apparition was seen. The licensee was in the cellar one day when the door to one of the unused alcoves opened to reveal the figure of a man wearing a doublet, breeches and stockings, typical costume of the seventeenth century and of the type which would have been worn by Rupert Nevill.

To get into the Wig & Pen Club in the Strand, one needs to be a gentleman of law or a member of the Press, but it is possible to visit the place by appointment should the reader so desire.

This club, one of the few building to have survived the Great Fire of London in 1666, lies opposite the Law Courts and is thought to be built on Roman remains. It has had quite a varied history, being in turn a shop, a private residence and solicitors' offices. It was also a keeper's cottage once upon a time, during which Cromwell's head was spiked on the top of Temple Bar: one night a gale blew the head off the Bar and into the cottage.

The present proprietor has often found it necessary to sleep on the empty premises and has been puzzled – usually around two o'clock in the morning – by the sound of footsteps walking along a corridor on the ground floor. It is thought that the footsteps are those of a solicitor who was found dead in his office one morning in the mid-1850s. Often they have been heard by members and staff on a Saturday afternoon – this is not so strange when one remembers that in the old days the solicitors kept their offices open six full days a week, unlike today.

The historic city of York boasts an interesting haunted pub, The Cock & Bottle Inn, which stands on the site of the much older Plumber's Arms, demolished some time ago. Who built the older pub is not really known, but it stood in the grounds of a large house in Bishophill, just off Micklegate.

George Villiers, second Duke of Buckingham, stayed here at some time and used it as a centre for alchemy in his efforts to turn base metals into gold. The odds are that he also dabbled in the 'black arts', for he certainly appears to have left some evil influences behind him. Despite being a favourite at the Court of King Charles II, he died a disgraced pauper. He spent his last years in York but it was actually at Kirkby Moorside that he died, his body being taken to Westminster for burial in a pauper's grave, although his ghost was to return to the York that he loved.

Over the years some very frightening events have taken place at the Cock & Bottle Inn, besides the more mundane opening and closing of doors, bangs and thumps, footsteps and the inevitable cold draughts. A man wearing a wide-brimmed Cavaliertype hat has been seen quite often, who suddenly evaporates, and anyone wearing a crucifix on the premises is likely to have it roughly snatched from them by unseen hands. I was told some time ago that one man was seized by an invisible force in an upstairs passage and pinned to the spot for several minutes, during which time he saw the apparition of a milkmaid carrying a yoke and buckets. Some time in 1972 a skeleton was found nearby on the site of the Duke of Buckingham's library, which might help to explain the hauntings in some way.

About thirty-seven miles to the south-west of York lies the village of Haworth, mecca of all Brontë-lovers. Here one will find the Weaver's Restaurant, formerly known as the Toby Jug, which boasts the ghost of the novelist Emily Brontë, who was brought up at the parsonage less than a hundred yards away.

Emily's ghost is said to appear each year on the anniversary of her death, 19 December. She was first reported as being seen in 1966, when the owners saw a small figure in a crinoline dress, carrying a wicker basket and smiling and giggling, cross the room to where the staircase used to be and climb up to the bedroom above. She was recognized as Emily Brontë from the portrait painted by her brother Branwell which still hangs in the parsonage museum.

Also at Haworth, the Sun Inn was said to be haunted for many years. The interior was altered somewhat during the early 1970s, and when it was re-opened, the new landlord was told of the ghost by the locals. He was very sceptical but, just to be on the safe side, he had a good-luck charm, in the shape of a gargoyle, placed over the door. All the whiskey in Yorkshire will not induce him to say whether this has been a success or not.

A couple of miles outside Haworth, on the B6250 road leading towards the Lancashire border, stands the tiny village of Stanbury. Just outside the village on the left-hand side of the road, silent and lonely, is the Olde Silent Inn, a beautiful old inn formerly known as The Eagle but better known as the place where, with a price on his head, Bonnie Prince Charlie was given food and shelter. One can still see the trapdoor through which the Young Pretender is said to have dropped onto a conveniently placed horse to make good his escape, as his pursuers hammered at the door.

However, it is not the ghost of the young Charles Stuart which haunts this lovely old inn but the soothing spectre of a former landlady, a sweet and kindly old soul who strokes the forehead of fretful sleepers. She was a lovely old dear who used to feed the many wild cats which once roamed these moors, calling them for their food by ringing a small bell. Folk in these parts say that she can still be heard at times, her little bell tinkling in the distance, soft and gentle like the sound of fairy bells being carried on a gentle breeze.

Warwickshire is Shakespeare country, and every year thousands of tourists visit that shrine of English literature Stratford-upon-Avon. A great many of them stay at the Ettington Park Hotel at Stratford, little realizing that this historic building, once known as Ettington Court and standing in about forty acres of magnificent country, is haunted.

Ettington, mentioned in the Domesday Book as Eatendone, is the original ancestral home of the Shirleys, one of England's oldest families. It is the third manor house to have stood on this site; the original was Saxon and the second Tudor, which was more or less re-built during the eighteenth and nineteenth centuries. The forty-bedroomed hotel retains its own private chapel and coach house, which until recent times housed the Shirleys' coach. To gain admission into the chapel, one has to pass through a concealed door in the dining-room, and there is another concealed door which leads from the ballroom into the library.

The cloister-like terrace beside the main entrance is the site of the majority of hauntings at Ettington. Several times the figure of a woman in a long white dress has been seen, nearly always at dusk, gliding along a tile-floored corridor, into which the family motto – '*Loyal je suis*' – is inscribed in mosaic tiling. Other incidents claimed to have been reported over the years, include the opening and closing of doors by unseen hands, in the old servants' quarters, situated in the turret rooms. Although the identity of the woman is unknown, she is believed to be associated with some family crime committed over 200 years ago, an incident which led to the 'bloody hand' being incorporated into the Shirley heraldic crest.

Ten miles to the north-east of Stratford, on the A46 road, is the town of Royal Leamington Spa, where a couple of miles from the railway station on Newland Road will be found the Jack & Jill Inn.

Several years ago a licensee, Mr Boulton, used to sit on the roof over the patio with his dog during warm summer evenings. In due course Mr Boulton died and in a short time he was almost forgotten, save by some of the older regular customers of the inn. In 1971 the then landlord was gazing out of his bedroom window on a still and humid June evening and saw the figure of a man, standing on the patio roof. He described him as being 'like the reflection of a television picture on glass, yet the window was open'. The description of the apparition, according to locals, seemed to fit that of the former licensee.

A few weeks later a barmaid, checking on bottles in the cellar, was terrified at seeing the shadowy figure of a man moving silently around the barrels. What scared her even more was that the barrels could be clearly seen through the apparition. Again the description tallied with that of the late Mr Boulton.

Seven miles from the centre of Oxford and its dreaming spires lies Woodstock with its twelfth-century Bear Inn, a lovely old inn which boasts a haunted bedroom and is an ideal stopping-off place for the ghost-hunting tourist.

When booking in, ask to be put into bedroom 16, where previous occupants have found their possessions moved around and heard footsteps, with other evidence of unseen occupants in the room. In 1967 an actress, whilst making a film in the area, stayed in bedroom 16. From the very first night her sleep was disturbed by footsteps on the creaking floorboards. Once, in the middle of the night, she awakened to find the dressing-table light switched on.

Other people have asked to be moved out of the room after only one night, and the manager related to me recently that over the past few years several people have complained of inexplicable happenings taking place in room 16.

About four miles from Oxford railway station stands a former fifteenth-century coaching house, the White Hart, now a busy modern pub. Like so many of these intriguing old pubs, this one also has a non-paying guest, a ghost called affectionately 'Rosalind'.

She has been seen frequently and her activities have been experienced over a period of several years. The phantom, wearing a veil and appearing to be crying bitterly, has been seen in the old brewery room, close to the site of an old spiral staircase which led to a loft. Rumour has it that this is the ghost of a girl who suffered from unrequited love and committed suicide by hanging herself from the old spiral staircase.

Amongst the many incidents associated with the sorrowful figure has been the tipping over of a barrel of sherry, numerous glasses being swept from the shelves at the back of the bar, and a hand-bell, used by the landlord for calling 'time', thrown to the floor.

For many tourists from overseas, the gateway to Britain is Manchester International Airport. Greater Manchester, Lancashire and Cheshire provide many haunted sites, including some well-known haunted inns.

The Ring O'Bells at Middleton in Greater Manchester is haunted by a Cavalier from the Civil War period, a rather sad-looking ghost, dressed in a plumed hat, lace collar and cloak and carrying a sword. Footsteps have been heard in the cellars, which date back to Norman times, and not so many years ago the flagstones were dug up, and helmets and weapons were found beneath them, dating back to the Civil War. Some human bones were also found which are thought to be those of a Royalist killed by Cromwell's troops whose ghost now haunts the pub.

Of the few people who have seen him, one was a lady who lived in a nearby cottage. She said she saw him very early one morning, a tall figure in the dress of the period. Former tenants of the inn report that he has made his presence known many, many times, thinking nothing of clapping a customer on the shoulder from behind, to the great consternation of the person concerned. Once, in a bar, a voice was heard laughing heartily, appearing to come out of thin air.

On the ground floor immediately over the cellar is a small room known as 'the snug'. In this room the ghosts of long dead

Cavaliers are believed to sit at night, just as they sat in secret conference over 300 years ago. Contained in this small room is what is known as 'the Cavalier's seat', and many people have complained of unusual coldness when sitting there, even when the room itself has been warm.

Right in the centre of Manchester stands the Shakespeare Hotel in Fountain Street, just off Piccadilly. This ancient inn is where the city's visiting show-business personalities gather. The Shakespeare is haunted by the ghost of a former servant girl who, about a hundred years ago, was killed after her clothing caught fire in the kitchen. In her panic she rushed to the top of the stairs before being overcome and falling headlong to her death. Her ghost is seen quite often near the stairs, by both staff and customers.

Still in Greater Manchester, at the Olde Rock House at Barton-on-Irwell, there is a ghost of a country yokel thrashing a flail and muttering, 'Now Thus. Now Thus', the motto of the de Trafford family. According to local historians, one of the de Traffords, fleeing Cromwell's troops, ran into the barn, grabbed a farmer's smock and put it on – along with an appropriate country bumpkin's expression – and joined in the corn threshing. Whether the disguise worked or not no one knows, but some years ago a flail and an old pile of clothes were found in a recess under the attic floor of the inn. For a long time they were exhibited in a glass case, as a reminder of the de Trafford whose ghost is still sighted from time to time, muttering, 'Now Thus. Now Thus.'

Over on Merseyside, the Adelphi Hotel on Liverpool's Lime Street is haunted by a friendly phantom. One girl who worked there recently told me that she woke up at about 5 a.m. on her first night at the hotel to find the figure of a man standing by her bed. At the time she was very frightened but she was told at breakfast, 'It was only George!' She told me, 'I have since found out that he is really quite friendly, but he is rather nosey.' No one seems to know what brings about these visitations – perhaps he just likes pretty girls.

Also in Liverpool, the Punch Bowl Inn at Sefton is said to be haunted by a seaman who died during the reign of Queen Elizabeth I. The mist-enshrouded figure of a young man has been seen floating several feet from the ground. Other people have seen the figure of a man dressed in sea-faring clothes sitting in a corner by the fireplace at the rear of a ground-floor room. Apparently this room was used many years ago as a mortuary for the bodies of sailors washed ashore, prior to their burial in Sefton churchyard, and the ghost is thought to be that of one of these drowned sailors.

One lady who saw the ghost was in an upstairs room at the inn on New Year's Eve 1973 when she saw the mist-enshrouded head and shoulders of a man seemingly floating in the air in front of her. She ran to the stairs to call a member of staff, but when they returned to the room, the figure had vanished. Another witness claims the ghost actually pushed her down the stairs.

Some of the regular customers told me of odd incidents which have taken place here over the years. One man insisted that he had been dragged from his bicycle in the pub car-park by an invisible assailant; another related how he was sitting in the bar one afternoon when someone came running in to say that a man, dressed in blue breeches like an old-fashioned sailor, was digging away at an unmarked grave in Sefton churchyard. Both men went out to see what he was up to and, on reaching the churchyard, discovered it was completely empty. But by the grave where the spectral figure had been seen digging there was a pile of fresh earth.

Cheshire boasts a fascinating ghost at the thirty-two-bedroomed Royal Hotel, which faces the Irish Sea on the Wirral Pensinsula ten miles across the River Mersey at Hoylake. The hotel, built in 1797, has an unidentified ghost who sports a Norfolk jacket, knickerbockers and tweed cap.

Several years ago there were frequent reports of an unknown spectre in one wing of the hotel, and in 1943 a female member of the staff reported seeing, on numerous occasions, a male figure in tweeds walking down the corridor from the hall towards the hotel ballroom. She described the man as being 'slight with an energetic and lively walk'. Twice she followed the solid-looking figure, but on both occasions it vanished inexplicably, and it was only afterwards that she realized that she had not noticed any sound accompanying the experience.

Some time later a barman said he saw a figure answering the same description pass from the billiards room and disappear along the corridor, where it was also witnessed by a colleague. The figure passed through the room where the barman stood, appearing to be solid and natural enough, yet, although he says he did not notice any sound, he did not think that the experience was altogether soundless.

A maintenance man on the hotel staff said he had seen a similar figure in the same room, many times, although his description did not entirely agree with those of other witnesses. Other inexplicable happenings include the opening and closing of doors, unexplained footsteps and the disappearance of small articles. The theory behind the haunting is that many years ago the body of a man was washed ashore at this point, having drowned in the Irish Sea, and instead of giving it a Christian burial, the mean proprietors of the hotel put the body back into the sea, to be carried out again by the tide. This was to bring back the spirit of the drowned man to haunt them forever, as a punishment for their tight-fistedness.

In the ancient city of Chester itself, the George & Dragon Inn, in Liverpool Road, is a comparatively modern pub built on the site of a 1,500-year-old Roman cemetery, and it is reputed to be haunted by what is said to be the steady, measured tread of a Roman soldier on 'eternal sentry duty'. Unexplained footsteps are sometimes heard pacing an upstairs floor of the pub, backwards and forwards, from one end to the other, in the early hours of the morning, seeming to pass through several solid brick walls in the process.

Just off the A1123 road, on the edge of the River Ouse, about ten miles east of Huntingdon, stands one of the best-known haunted inns in the country, the Ferry Boat Inn, which is built on a site that has been haunted for nearly a thousand years by the ghost of Juliet, a pretty young girl who fell in love with a dubious local character by the name of Tom Zoul. Juliet was infatuated by him, but Tom preferred the company of his drinking companions to hers, and she, neglected by him, was slowly breaking her heart. One day her grief became too much for her, so, wearing a pink dress which was a favourite of Tom's, she committed suicide by hanging herself from a tree beside the river, on the wild spring morning of 17 March. The Church would not allow Juliet to be buried in consecrated ground, but she was given a last resting-place near the river, her grave simply marked with a plain grey stone slab.

Several centuries passed and then along came the builder of the Ferry Boat Inn, and he decided to incorporate Juliet's gravestone in the floor of the inn, for he was short of stone and the nearest quarry was in the next county, several miles away. To this day it can still be seen, forming part of the floor of the inn, and for many years people have gathered here on 17 March to watch for Juliet's ghost, which is said to rise from the stone and drift out of the inn and down to the River Ouse.

Not many years ago, as many as 400 people turned up on the anniversary, but Juliet would not deign to make an exhibition of herself in front of so many people. She is the classic ghost which everyone knows about but which very few people can claim to have seen, although on several occasions odd occurrences have taken place. The pub dog refuses to go anywhere near the flagstone, and even in this enlightened age the local women still refuse to enter the inn round about the time of the anniversary.

During the Civil War, when the Parliamentarian troops were beginning to gain a stranglehold over the troops still loyal to the Crown, the port of Siddlesham, some five miles south of Chichester in Sussex, became perhaps the most important of the escape routes from this country for Royalists bound for France or Holland, and the inn which stood on the site of the present Crab & Lobster Inn became a centre of activity for Royalist underground activities.

When Chichester fell after a short siege by Cromwell's troops, there was a flurry of activity in Siddlesham, as isolated groups of Cavaliers broke through Roundhead lines and made for safety. Among them were Sir Robert Earnley, his two nephews and their companions. Whilst waiting at the inn for a boat to take them across the English Channel, they were surprised by a patrol of Roundheads and a running fight ensued in which all six Cavaliers were shot down in the roadway outside the inn – though some people say they were carried mortally wounded into the inn where they subsequently died.

Over the centuries there have been many reports of a tall figure, wearing the clothes of the Civil War period, seen both inside and outside the Crab & Lobster Inn. It was suggested that either those who made the sightings were drunk, or the landlord was capitalizing on the story, but in 1965-6 the hauntings became more credible, and brought tourists flocking to the area from all corners of the globe, as a result of one woman's experience.

First the pub cat began to behave rather strangely, particularly in the saloon bar, where it always appeared to avoid certain parts of the floor, often leaping onto a chair in terror, its fur standing on end, as if trying to avoid something which only it could see. One of the bedrooms had to be abandoned because of what was described as 'an inexplicably unpleasant atmosphere'. Heavy footsteps would be heard walking around downstairs during the night, but when the landlord went to investigate, everything was quiet and the doors and windows were properly secured.

During the summer of 1969 a man and his wife called at the inn for a meal, just as hundreds of visitors to the area do each year during the summer season. As the landlord led them through to the dining-room, the lady suddenly cried out and, standing transfixed, gazed into the saloon bar. Gathering herself together and without comment, she then went into the dining-room. Following lunch, she asked the landlord whether or not the inn was haunted, and when he enquired as to why she had put the question, she said that, as she had looked into the saloon bar on her way to the dining-room, she had seen a man in the costume of the Civil War period lying on the floor close to death and, with a small lace handkerchief, feebly trying to stem the flow of blood which spurted from a bullet hole in his chest.

Everyone else appeared to be unaware of it; in fact, people were actually sitting around him, quite close, drinking and chatting, totally oblivious of there being anything unusual.

For our final haunted hostelry, we go across to the West Country and the Crown Hotel in Poole, Dorset, an old inn which is believed to have housed at one time the notorious seventeenth-century Judge Jeffries – the 'Hanging Judge' – when he sat at the Assizes at the Guildhall, less than a hundred yards away.

In the 1960s the joint licensees decided they would try to attract a wider clientele by converting the upper floor of the stable block in the courtyard into a 'beat' club. The idea was quite new in those days, and the principle of mixing up-to-date beat groups with the antiquity of a bygone age seemed at the time a novel formula. Consequently they began to alter and modernize the old hayloft on the first floor.

In 1966 two men working in the new clubroom until closing time came down the old outside staircase into the courtyard, where they met and began to talk to some customers from the hotel bar. Suddenly the group heard a piano, which was stored in the old first-floor room, begin to play, as single notes were struck one at a time, as if a child or a person was hitting the keyboard at random with one finger. They all laughed when one of the group suggested, half-jokingly, that it was the ghost, and unsuspectingly they all trooped back up the stairs to see who was in the room. From the doorway, the whole of the room, including the old piano, could be seen at a glance – and it was completely empty, yet the piano continued to tinkle for several seconds before falling silent.

At that instant the hammers, nails and other tools which had been lying on the piano lid suddenly shot into the air, before crashing to the floor. The men beat a hasty retreat and stood in the courtyard, frightened and staring at the entrance to the stairway, half expecting some fearful apparition to emerge. What did manifest itself was perhaps more terrifying: it was a ball of fluorescent mist, about the size of a child's head, which, with a fine sense of the horrific, drifted from the doorway, glided past the speechless group and then floated out through the archway to vanish into nearby Market Street.

One of the joint licensees then complained of noises in the main part of the inn itself, sounding as if a heavy object or a body was being dragged across the upper floors, but for a time at least the stable block remained quiet. A week or so later the renovations were re-started, although the two or three men working up in the old hayloft jumped at the least noise and kept a wary eye on the room for the first sign of anything unusual. Half-way through the first evening's work, the door to the hayloft, which had been securely fastened, began to swing open slowly – and the men again ran.

A resident guest at the hotel poured scorn on the story. He was very sceptical and level-headed, believing the incidents to be purely imaginative. To prove the point, he asked for a can of paint and a brush and went up to the old room, where he painted five large crosses on the door, deliberately bolting it. He was not to remain a sceptic for very much longer. No sooner had he bolted the door than, before his own eyes, it again swung slowly open.

In 1974 the milkman, who normally left the bottles in the courtyard at the back door of the inn between five and six o'clock in the morning, told the licensees that in future he would leave them on the pavement in the street by the front entrance to the inn. When asked why, he said he was afraid of the sounds of children running and screaming in the stable block, which he knew was locked up and empty. Apparently, some time earlier one of the proprietors had also gone out, rather angrily, because he thought children were playing in the stable block late at night. After several calls which were ignored, and going into the stables, they were found to be empty, totally deserted.

No one really knows the origin of the haunting, although there is a vague rumour circulating in the area of a landlord, who many years ago, killed and buried two deformed children in the stable block. Whether this is true or whether it is contrived, I have been unable to discover, but the events which have taken place there over the years tend to add a certain fascination to this lovely old inn.

9. Knights of the High Toby

The sense of the supernatural can be very real on the roads of England today, despite the modern motorway system, sprawling suburbia and all the materialistic influences of an urban civilization. Possibly the best time for the ghost-hunting tourist to travel through the country is at night. Roads are empty for several miles on end; the countryside, rolling moorlands and fells take on a different guise when seen only beyond the range of the headlights. The familiar becomes unfamiliar, unknown places take on an air of non-approachability, for beyond the warmth and security of the car lies a world which is at once enticing and intimidating. But by comparison with the roads of 200 years ago, the modern roads of England are a haven of peace and safety.

The eighteenth and early nineteenth centuries – a period spanning 150 years – were the age of those self-styled 'Knights of the High Toby' – the highwaymen. They were rife along the main highways, although many in fact preferred the lonely roads and country lanes. It was to serve the stage-coaches that major highways such as the Great North Road were built, and they in turn were to serve the purposes of the highwayman admirably. The roads had an unsavoury reputation, and people travelled them at their peril. It was the coming of the railways – not better law-enforcement – which put the highwaymen out of business.

Many of the ghosts which today haunt the Queen's highways are those of men who were legends in their own lifetime, and folk have told terrifying tales ever since the highwaymen were a source of terror to travellers. Dick Turpin, of course, lends his name to many of the old pubs and inns along the Great North Road, and any room where Turpin and his cronies might possibly have hidden is almost certain to have a ghost story attached to it. Legend has made more of Dick Turpin than there really was. He was a coward, a cheat and a cruel thug. His greatest success was not as a highwayman but as a cattle-stealer, and he was hanged not for highway robbery but for stealing a horse.

To shatter the myth completely, it was not even Dick Turpin who rode the famous Black Bess from London to York in 1678, covering the distance in the incredible time of fifteen hours and thirty-five minutes to establish an alibi. This feat was carried out by one of Yorkshire's infamous sons, William Nevison.

Despite this feat on the famous black horse, Bess, Nevison was arrested and placed in York Castle, from where he managed to escape after bribing his gaoler. King Charles II offered a reward of £20 for his capture, and it was not long before he was caught and subsequently hanged on the York Tyburn. The ghost of William Nevison is said to haunt a copse known as 'Hanging Wood', at Ardwick-le-Street in North Yorkshire, where he pulled off most of his highway robberies. He also allegedly haunts the area around Batley, near Leeds, where in 1681 he was involved in a fight and killed a man called Darcy Fletcher.

Much more authentic are the stories of the highwayman's ghost to be seen at various points between Scotch Corner and Boroughbridge, about six miles south-east of the cathedral town of Ripon, in North Yorkshire. This ghost is without doubt that of Tom Hoggett, self-styled 'King of the High Tobymen of the Great North Road'.

Hoggett, like Turpin, was a real dyed-in-the-wool villain whose success at lifting purses over a wide area earned him quite a reputation. Eventually he was caught by troopers sent out from York, at the Salutation Inn one stormy, moonless night, and kept under guard until he could be taken back to York on the mailcoach the following day. The ever-resourceful Hoggett bided his time and during the night was able to escape from his captors. He made a dash for the nearby River Swale, hoping to cross it at Langdon Fords, but in the darkness he stumbled into a deep pond and drowned.

The pond still bears his name, and many stories are told of how, on moonless and stormy nights, Hoggett's ghostly figure can be seen, hatless and wearing a caped coat reaching to his ankles, gliding alongside the road at considerable speed, his coat glowing feebly, as if illuminated by a dim lantern.

About eight or nine miles from the ancient town of Clitheroe, in Lancashire's beautiful Ribble Valley, a ghostly highwayman can be found at the Punch Bowl Inn in the hamlet of Hurst Green. This is the well-known spectre of Ned King, who confined his talents to the area between Longridge and Clitheroe, making the Punch Bowl his headquarters. Here, from the safety of the hayloft above the barn, he could size up his potential victims, moneyed gentlemen and their ladies, as they alighted from the coach to take refreshments whilst the horses were changed. After being refreshed, the victims would return to their coach, and as they drove away, Ned King would be waiting for them with pistols drawn, a mile or so down the road. Having relieved them of their valuables, he would then make his escape across the fields, back to the Punch Bowl. Eventually his luck ran out, he was betrayed and the troopers sent out from Preston finally caught up with him in his hide-out above the barn. He shot it out for a while but eventually ran out of ammunition and after a brief struggle was overpowered.

The barn is now the inn's restaurant and one can see, on the right-hand side of what is today the minstrels' gallery, the spot where Ned King was captured. In those days justice was swift. For Ned King punishment was even swifter, for he was taken from the inn in chains and without trial or further ado was hanged from a gibbet which stood not far from the front door of the old inn, a spot past which he must have galloped on his way to and from his many hold-ups.

For well over 150 years the ghost of Ned King has haunted both the Punch Bowl Inn and the area around Hurst Green, his trusty steed often glimpsed as it silently speeds him across the fields away from the site of one of his many hold-ups.

The Lancashire industrial town of Bolton is usually associated with the cotton industry and with Samuel Crompton, the inventor of the 'spinning-mule'. Not far from Crompton's old home runs Belmont Road, once the haunt of a notorious highwayman by the name of Horrocks.

One night, having held up the Manchester stage-coach, Horrocks was surprised by the sudden arrival of a young traveller called Grimshaw, and in his haste to get away he threw the booty into the bushes and marked the spot, intending to return for it when the coast was clear. However, the young Grimshaw saw a piece of jewellery glistening in the moonlight and, on investigation, discovered the proceeds of the robbery. Instead of handing the property over to the authorities as soon as possible, the young man kept it, in the hope of turning it into easy money. However, he made the mistake of trying to sell some of the jewellery from the haul in a local tavern, where he was seen by a thief-taker and arrested. He was sent up before the magistrate and charged with highway robbery. At his subsequent trial, his story about finding the stolen goods was disbelieved and he was found guilty and hanged at Preston in 1780.

It is the ghost of the young Grimshaw that is now said to haunt Belmont Road, with a piece of the gallows-rope around his neck, his eyes popping out of his head, trying to protest his innocence although no words come out of the gaping mouth, and no sound is heard, as he roams the area on dark nights.

John Whitfield was a native of Cotehill in Cumbria, a notorious and much-feared highwayman who in 1768 shot and killed a man in cold blood after robbing him on the Carlisle-Penrith road. Unknown to him, a small boy hiding nearby had witnessed the whole incident and he was able to give enough information to the authorities to lead to Whitfield's arrest and conviction for murder.

Because of his notoriety, Whitfield was not executed by hanging in the normal way but is said to have been gibbeted alive. He suffered a dreadful death and it is recorded that before his life was terminated he hung in appalling agony and suffering for many days, until a passing coachman, out of pity, put an end to the man's misery and suffering with a bullet. Over the years, many travellers have testified that Whitfield's cries are still heard as they pass that spot at Barrock on the Carlisle-Penrith road.

Twelve miles from Berwick-on-Tweed in Northumberland, running almost parallel with the A1 main trunk road, is a country road which links the villages of Buckton and Fenwick. Just outside Buckton there is a group of trees, well known as the haunt of a ghostly figure in a dark cloak, which has been observed walking around for several minutes before simply vanishing, as if into thin air.

This is said to be the ghost not of a highwayman but of a female counterpart, the daughter of Sir John Cochrane. According to the history books, Sir John was sentenced to death in 1685 for supporting the Duke of Argyll, and his daughter, Griselle, decided on a bold attempt to stop the execution. She disguised herself as a highwayman and held up the mailcoach carrying the death warrant. She was successful in this scheme, and the action was sufficient to cause enough delay and thus enable Sir John's friends to arrange a pardon for him.

Perhaps the best known of all female highway robbers was Lady Katherine Ferrers who, in the eighteenth century, lived a double life. She was admirably re-created by filmstar Margaret Lockwood in a film loosely based on Lady Ferrers' life, *The Wicked Lady*.

During the day, often accompanied by her unsuspecting husband, she would enjoy the normal social life of a titled lady of the period. But at night she would don the clothes and character of a highwayman, and for a few years she successfully robbed night travellers, often selecting her victims from guests her husband had innocently invited to dinner earlier in the evening. She was said to be more vicious towards her own sex than towards the handsome young gentry – who often took her fancy, and on a couple of her exploits she was said to have been in the company of another highwayman. Eventually she was shot in a running fight with the law, but she was able to reach home and her bedroom before collapsing. Now her secret was revealed, a few hours before she died.

All this action took place on Nomansland Common at St Albans in Hertfordshire where there stands a pub, the Wicked Lady, named after Lady Ferrers and believed to have been used by her for illicit meetings with her nightly companions. Her ghost is thought to haunt the pub, although it is more often met outside on the common. The last time it was encountered was, to my knowledge, in December 1970, when the landlord of the pub was walking his dog late one night. He later told the local newspaper that he heard the sound of a horse galloping at high speed through the shrubland. It came so close, he said, that he could have touched it, but nothing could be seen, not even a movement of the bushes. Yet it took a great deal of soothing to quieten his dog, which had been scared out of its wits by the phantom horse.

Also in Hertfordshire, about two miles from Knebworth railway station, are Bramfield Road and Whitehorse Lane.

In the eighteenth century a regular visitor to the local fairs and markets was a renowned pie-man by the name of Clibbon. He seemed an affable sort of person, who showed a keen interest in the movements and activities of local farmers. However, after talking to him, residents in the area were a little disturbed to learn of the successful exploits of a highwayman who had been robbing farmers returning from the sales at the market. The disturbing number of coincidences came to an abrupt end when the highwayman was finally caught – in the Bull's Green area of Bramfield Road – and revealed to be the friendly pie-man. The farmers were naturally incensed with rage at Clibbon's deceit, a friend and drinking companion in the morning and robbing them of their money in the evening. After giving him a severe beating, they tied him to a horse and allowed it to drag his half-conscious body for many yards before finally finishing him off.

In recent years, people passing the area in the evenings have reported seeing the vague shape of a horse pulling a 'writhing body' along the lanes, and they have heard the moans of the ghostly Clibbon as he continues, after nearly 200 years, to plead for mercy. Some have heard only what they consider to be the sounds of the incident, the horse's hooves and the scattering of gravel, accompanied by the weird, unearthly moans of the highwayman.

The ruins of a Franciscan monastery at Winchelsea, near Rye in Sussex, were once the home of two well-known highwaymen.

The brothers Joseph and George Weston lived here under

assumed names and were looked upon by the locals as country gentleman, but at night they donned cape, mask and tricorn hat and plied their trade as 'Knights of the High Toby' throughout the surrounding countryside. They were caught in London after robbing the Bristol mailcoach and were subsequently executed at Tyburn in 1783.

But according to local observers, the two brothers are still to be seen in the ruins of their former home, or careering about the district at dead of night. One, believed to be George, is often sighted in the shadows of a particular tree, armed but, by all accounts, headless, and waiting for the opportunity to surprise and rob a phantom stage-coach. Many motorists claim to have been frightened by the sounds of galloping horses' hooves, seeming to come up on them from behind, which, on reaching them, cease as mysteriously as they begin.

Does Dick Turpin haunt any stretch of the Queen's highway?

He does. He has been identified as the ghost seen on Watling Street (the A5) between Hinckley and Nuneaton. The ghost seen here wears a large black tricorn hat and, rather unusual for a ghost seen in the dark, he is said to wear a coat with sleeves of such a brilliant red that the colour is easily noted if there is a moon, or if car headlights illuminate the figure before it fades.

Another village where Turpin can be observed from time to time is Wroughton-on-the-Green, a village which sits alongside the River Ouse on the B488 road between Newport Pagnell and Bletchley in Buckinghamshire. The figure, cloaked and hazy, moves about restlessly and with no apparent wish to move far away, something which suggests the ghost is impatiently waiting for something to happen. History confirms that Turpin did indeed use this village as a hide-away after his exploits a couple of miles across the fields, on Watling Street. In fact, it was at the Swan Inn at Wroughton that he forced the blacksmith at gunpoint to reverse the shoes on his horse to confound his pursuers.

South of Waltham, where the A11 Norwich-London road runs through Epping Forest, is another stretch said to be haunted by Turpin, and the stretch just to the north of the forest is haunted by perhaps the nastiest but most characteristic of all his spectres. Mounted on a black horse, it gallops at breakneck speed along the road with a skinny woman clutching at its waist and hanging down with feet touching the ground. She shrieks mournfully.

Again, we know from documents of the period that, when Turpin heard of an aged and wealthy widow living on her own on the outskirts of Loughton, he waylaid her one evening when she was out walking, tortured her until she revealed where she had hidden her jewellery and then dragged her behind his horse until she was battered to death.

There was nothing in the least romantic about Dick Turpin.

Of course, there are other ghosts to be met on the roads of England, besides those of highwaymen. The bitterness of the Civil War has left traditions and hauntings scattered up and down the country, and many of the sites of some of the major battles have tales of hauntings about them. In fact, a great many of the ghosts seen on the highways of England are relics from the Civil War.

The A422 road from Alderminster to Banbury borders an area where one of the most notable ghostly scenes was ever recorded – the battlefield of Edgehill, seven miles outside Banbury.

Within a year of the battle of Edgehill, a pamphlet was published describing the re-appearance of troops who fought and perished in this first great battle of the Civil War in 1642. Witnesses included several clergymen and several Army officers who had actually recognized some of the combatants.

According to testimonies witnessed by a Justice of the Peace, on the Christmas Eve following the battle local people heard the sounds of distant drums, accompanied by shouts, the crash of musket fire and all the noise of battle. Then suddenly there appeared in the air battalions of soldiers with flags flying, drums beating and infantry discharging small arms and cannon. The phantom battle is said to have continued for upwards of two hours until the Royalists took flight, and soon after the apparitions vanished. The next night people from the surrounding district went to Edgehill and witnessed for themselves the same dreadful vision.

After several more sightings, news reached the King, who was then at Oxford. King Charles was sufficiently impressed to send six officers, headed by Colonel Lewis Kirke to make enquiries. They visited the hilly ridge themselves the following Saturday and Sunday and saw the same vision. Some of Kirke's brother officers claimed to have seen the faces of some of the Royalists so clearly that they recognized comrades who had died in the battle.

Rarely has a year passed since this memorable event without a few people visiting Edgehill in the hope of seeing the spectral hosts again. They go there on 12 October, the anniversary of the battle, and at Christmas weekends, but apart from vague sounds of horses neighing and glimpses of peculiar lights in the sky above the battleground, no confirmed reports of sightings have been forthcoming.

On 2 July 1644 Cromwell again defeated a Royalist army under Prince Rupert, at the great débâcle of Marston Moor, just under a mile away from the village of Long Marston, near Wetherby in North Yorkshire. Ever since that terrible day, tales of ghostly Cavaliers fighting it out with Roundheads have been told. Some people claimed, as at Edgehill, to have seen the battle silhouetted in the sky, whilst others tell of seeing ghost survivors trudging by the wayside.

In November 1932 two touring motorists, lost in their search for the Wetherby road, found themselves travelling along the A59 Skipton road, which cuts right through the site of the old battlefield. Ahead of them they noticed a small group of perhaps three or four ragged individuals, stumbling silently along the ditch. Realizing there was something odd about them, they slowed down to look more closely. The figures were dressed as Cavaliers, with wide-brimmed hats turned up and fastened with cockades, and long, flowing locks. At first the motorists thought they must have been actors from some carnival event.

The figures, moving in the same direction as the car, with their backs to it, suddenly staggered to the centre of the road and into the path of bus approaching from the opposite direction. It was obvious the driver of the bus could not see them, as he did not even slow down and appeared to the two observers to plough straight through them. They stopped the car and searched the road on either side, but they were unable to find a trace of anyone. Today one still hears of people witnessing solitary figures haunting the battleground.

Apparitions on such a large scale as those at Edgehill and Marston Moor which appear to so many people, are, of course, rare, and there are many people today who believe that over the years the stories have been added to and grossly exaggerated. But perhaps the story told by two reliable and respectable witnesses in the 1950s might suggest that the old accounts might not be so much of an exaggeration after all.

In July 1951 two women – a nurse and an accountant – were holidaying at the Luttrell Arms Hotel in Dunster, Somerset. Making this ancient inn their headquarters they were able to explore the usual tourist attractions of the town and castle, following which they began to go for walks further afield. One day they decided to go to Conygar Hill, a few miles to the north of Dunster, a circular battlemented tower standing on a steep mound, whose slopes are covered with trees and shrubs. The gradient was much steeper than the two ladies had at first realized, and it was only by hauling themselves up by the branches of small trees and shrubs that they finally reached the top, breathless and exhausted. However, the view from the summit, a great circle of green Somerset countryside, and a cloudless blue sky of a blazing July day, made the effort well worthwhile. Fascinated by the lovely sight which spread out before them, they slipped into the tower and climbed to the top for an even better panoramic view, which they found intoxicating.

After some time they came back down, and as they stood outside the tower again, they became aware that something was different. A change seemed to have taken place in the atmosphere during the time they had been on top of the tower. The sun still beat down from a cloudless sky, yet strangely a bitterly cold wind wrapped around them as if it was a winter's day. Both ladies felt uneasy, not only because of the cold wind, for which there seemed no natural reason, and they both turned in the direction of a faint but unmistakable sound of a large group of people, seemingly marching towards them.

They now began to feel frightened, for they both knew that, even if there had been no undergrowth or bushes on the slope, it was far too steep for anyone to walk up at the speed of these marching footsteps. Even so, the rhythmic tread seemed to be coming along a horizontal path at their own level, and in their minds there was no doubting the fact that they were about to be overwhelmed by an invisible phantom army. The marching steps came nearer and nearer, the wind seeming to increase as they did so, until the trees on the hillside began to sway. The gloom appeared to thicken, and then, just when the invisible spectral troops were almost level, the women were overtaken with terror and plunged in almost suicidal haste down the steep embankment, not stopping, despite torn clothing and gashes from the shrubland, until they reached the safety of the road below.

It was only then that they stopped and breathlessly looked back up towards the tower. The hot sun beat down on them, the air was still and the tower shimmered in the heat. The trees and shrubs were still and the air around was calm and silent – and of the marching feet there was not a sound. Nor was there an explanation.

During the Civil War there were some bitter engagements here, when Dunster Castle was held by both sides at various times, but there was never, to my knowledge, any major battle here such as at Edgehill or Marston Moor. However, just to the east stands Sedgemoor, scene of a bitter and bloody battle during the Monmouth rebellion of 1683. So who can say whose marching footsteps these might have been. Cavaliers? Roundheads? Or maybe they were the the footsteps of rebelling peasants.

Shropshire has no such ghostly spectacles. It was by comparison lightly touched by pitched battle in the Civil War, although many bloody skirmishes were fought around the county. Perhaps the best-known incident which took place here was between the Parliamentarian troops and the Royalists led by Major Smalman of Wilderhope Manor at Church Stretton, thirteen miles south of Shrewsbury.

Smalman was a dogmatic, irascible and fanatical Royalist, who, after killing a relative in a duel, because he supported the wrong side, became an obvious target for Roundheads mopping up pockets of resistance when the power of King Charles was on the verge of collapse. In 1645 the Major's house, Wilderhope Manor, was surrounded and put under siege by Roundheads. In the confusion he managed to escape, but he was spotted as he galloped away across the wild country of Wenlock Edge and was immediately pursued. On reaching Blakeway Coppice, Smalman suddenly swung his horse to the left and leapt over the edge of the escarpment which plunged over ninety feet. Convinced that such a fall must be fatal, the pursuing Roundheads abandoned the chase and returned to the looting of Wilderhope Manor. But the wily Smalman was not finished yet. He had managed to end up, bruised and dishevelled, in a crab-apple tree, although his horse had plunged to its death below.

In 1965 two London art lecturers who were approaching retirement passed through the small village of Enchmarsh one bright and sunny April afternoon. As they approached the top of a rise, travelling very slowly to take in the magnificent scenery, they were suddenly delighted by the appearance of a large black horse, standing sideways in the middle of the track, just ahead of them. The rider wore the wide-brimmed, large plumed hat, cloak and breeches of a seventeenth-century nobleman and seemed not to have noticed the approaching car. He sat motionless on his horse, his clothes moving in the hilltop breeze, staring intently to the west.

The couple slowed the car to a halt, and both watched silent and fascinated as, still without any hint of consciousness of the car, horse and rider leapt into the field on the left-hand side of the track, turned sharply and then galloped southwards, parallel to the roadway. The couple followed their progress as long as they were visible, and then, starting the car engine, continued on their own way. Discussing the event later, they were struck by the fact that both horse and rider were colourless, just greys and blacks similar to a monochrome photograph, with only the feather of his hat standing out in vivid white. Another point which struck them was that, although the car windows were open, they heard no sound, even though the horse and rider galloped past just a few yards away from them.

Had they in fact witnessed Major Smalman's ghost, making his escape from Wilderhope Manor? Certainly the area where he was seen is near to his old home, and it is probable that, when he escaped in 1645, he would certainly have preferred to head north-west towards the wilder country of Wales for a hiding-place, rather than north-east, back into Parliamentarian territory.

The roads of Old England abound with an astonishing variety of ghosts: highwaymen, Roman soldiers, phantom coaches, spectral omnibuses and even ghostly hitch-hikers. These ghosts or spirits have come back across hundreds of years in many cases, but none has come further than the phantom horseman who rides the north Dorset countryside, for he is thought to date back some 2,500 years to the Bronze Age, which gives him the dubious distinction of being perhaps the oldest ghost in Europe.

The ghostly horseman usually puts in his appearances close to the A3081 road which runs between Sixpenny Handley and Cranbourne, a beautiful part of the West Country which today is mainly quiet and devoted to agriculture. Thousands of years ago it was different: it was a hive of Bronze Age activity. The fields around here are dotted with ancient burial mounds and a strange earthworks, known as the Cursus, which runs across the fields for about six miles. The Cursus is really two parallel ditches running about seventy-five yards apart, and it is here that the horseman is usually seen. His ghostly rides have become a legend as over the years farmers and shepherds have reported seeing him galloping across the fields towards the Cursus.

In the late 1920s he terrified two young girls as they cycled from Handley to Cranborne one night, appearing from nowhere and riding alongside them for some considerable distance before disappearing. But it was a few years earlier that the most documented sighting was made.

Mr R.C. Clay was the leader of a team of archaeologists at the time excavating a Bronze Age settlement near Christchurch in Dorset, and he came face to face with the horseman when, in 1924 he was driving from the site to his home in Salisbury in Wiltshire. As he passed a spot where an old Roman road crossed the modern highway, he saw a horseman galloping across the fields ahead of him. The horseman was going flat out towards the road, and as Mr Clay slowed down to let him cross, the rider swung his horse round and galloped parallel to the vehicle, some forty yards away.

For over a hundred yards the horseman kept pace with the car, whilst Mr Clay watched fascinated. In spite of his surprise, he managed to take in a great deal of detail of both horse and rider. He noted that the horse was no bigger than a pony, with a long tail and mane, and it had neither bridle nor stirrups. The rider had bare legs and a long flowing cloak and was holding some sort of weapon above his head. As suddenly as it had appeared, the apparition vanished. Mr Clay stopped the car, trying to gather his thoughts. His first instinct was to get out and look round, but as it was getting dark, he decided to press on home.

The following morning he was back to see if he could discover anything which might explain his ghostly encounter. He searched the road and surrounding area for several hundred yards on either side of the spot but found nothing – nothing, that is, except a low burial mound almost exactly where the spectral horeman had disappeared. However, his one encounter with the ghostly horseman, coupled with his own expert knowledge, enabled him to date the figure as from the late Bronze Age – somewhere between 700 and 600 BC.

Another ancient ghost, possibly nearly as old as the phantom horseman but much more horrifying, is said to terrify victims on Dartmoor in Devon.

A young woman in her mid-twenties was driving across Dartmoor along the lonely stretch of road from Postbridge to Two Bridges, after a sightseeing tour, when the car started to judder. She pulled over to the side of the road to look at the handbook, and as she was reading in the failing light, she said she felt a cold feeling suddenly come over her and felt as if she was being watched. Nervously looking up, she saw, to her absolute horror, a pair of huge, hairy hands pressed against the windscreen. She watched terrified as the disembodied hands began to crawl across the windscreen and, after what seemed to be a lifetime, she finally managed to scream, at which point they suddenly vanished.

This 'curse' that has terrified victims on Dartmoor for over sixty years first began to be felt in the 1920s. Pony traps were overturned, cyclists felt their handlebars wrenched from their grasp, causing them to run full tilt into stone walls, horses shied and bolted, and a doctor travelling on a motorcycle with two children in the sidecar was nearly killed when the engine literally detached itself from the machine. An army officer reported an enormous pair of hands covered in long, dark hairs taking charge of his steering-wheel, covering his own. But things finally reached a head in 1921, when a newspaper sent some intrepid investigators to the spot, and the local authority had the camber of the road altered. Even so, the hands refused to be deterred.

Just after the road improvements were finished, a young couple were visiting the area with their caravan. As is common on Dartmoor, a heavy fog suddenly enveloped the area as they were driving towards Plymouth one evening. Rather than drive on and risk losing their way, the couple decided to park in a lay-by on the Postbridge road. After cooking a light meal they settled down to sleep, to enable them to make an early start the following morning.

The woman had been asleep for only a short time when she was awakened by a strange scratching noise which seemed to be coming from outside the caravan. Thinking it might be a dog wandering lost on the moors, she got out of bed to have a look. Suddenly a strange chill came over her, and for some reason she felt compelled to look at the window above her sleeping husband's bunk. There, slowly crawling across the glass right above her husband, was an enormous pair of hairy hands. The poor woman was too stunned even to cry out, but as she sat rigid with fear she made the sign of the cross – and the hands vanished.

In 1960 the hands were thought to have been the reason behind a fatal crash on this lonely stretch of road, when a motorist driving from Plymouth to Chagford was found dead beneath the wreckage of his overturned car. No other car was involved and there seemed to be no reason, other than a fault in the car itself, that could have caused the vehicle to career off the road. But when police experts examined the wreckage, they could find no mechanical fault in the car. It is a mystery which so far has not been solved.

Motorists are not the only ones to have been victims of the

hairy-hand phenomena. Walkers making their way along this stretch of road have reported strange experiences and sensations, even though they have been unaware of the legend of the hands. One hiker enjoying the rugged scenery got carried away during his walk and found himself making his way along the road at dusk. Suddenly he was overcome by an inexplicable feeling of panic which rooted him to the spot. Minutes later the feeling passed and he continued on his way, puzzling over his strange experience.

No one can explain the phenomena and the strange happenings on this lonely stretch of road. The only possible clue might lie in the fact that, in the far and distant past, a Bronze Age village stood along the once busy but now sinister Dartmoor road.

One ghost the reader might be thankful to meet can be found on the A64 road between Pickering and York: her sole aim appears to be to help travellers in distress.

Nance was a farmer's daughter from Sheriff Hutton who was engaged to be married to a mailcoach driver on the York-Berwick run. Unfortunately, in the case of Nance, absence failed to make the heart grow fonder, and she found solace in the arms of another man, eventually running off with him. About a year later, the coachman was shocked to find her one cold wet night waiting at the side of the road with a baby in her arms. She was so weak and ill she could hardly stand.

Stopping the coach, he lifted her and the baby into the seat beside him, and as they continued on their journey to York, the girl told him what had happened to her over the past year. It appears that the lover had abandoned her when the child was born, and not only had he been a married man, he was also a highwayman to boot.

The coachman took Nance and her child to the Black Swan Inn in Coney Street in York, but both she and the child died during the night from exhaustion and starvation.

Some years later the coachman, now nearing retirement, was again approaching York when he ran into dense fog, forcing him to send a postillion to lead the horses at a snail's pace. Suddenly the reins were jerked into the air by invisible hands, and the horses set off into the fog at a frantic gallop. Looking round in terror, the coachman saw Nance seated beside him whipping the horses on, dressed as she had been on the night she died. She drove the horses flat out into York and into the yard of the Black Swan.

Nance can still be found on the A64 road, particularly on foggy nights: a lithe, young, ragged girl, moving swiftly in the glare of the headlights. Any driver who cares to trust her can be confident that, for as long as he can see her, he is safe. She will glide faster when the road ahead is clear and will slow down should there be hidden dangers ahead – the cats' eyes in the centre of the road gleaming clear through her emaciated body.

Deep in the beautiful and winding Manifold Valley in Staffordshire stand the remains of Throwley Hall, one-time residence of Oliver Cromwell's family. Today, like some of the ruins old Nol knocked about, there is very little left of the place, except for a couple of walls and a heap of stone and rubble. But even so, today's visitors tell of feeling an atmosphere about the place which is difficult to define. One has the feeling of foreboding as though the place has some ghastly crime to hide – which, in a way, it has.

During the time of Cromwell, some members of the family went to Ashbourne, about six miles away, in the family coach. The coachman was given orders to pick them up again in the early evening and was sent back to the Hall. Early in the afternoon a torrential storm unleashed itself, and the valley was shrouded in thick cloud, whilst the road from the Hall soon became a quagmire.

The coachman, whilst under orders, was naturally reluctant to go back to Ashbourne for the family. Nevertheless, he set off, his horses slithering and sliding in the mud, the coach lurching from side to side, and eventually the steaming team arrived at Ashbourne where, after picking up the party, the coachman lost no time in setting off back to Throwley Hall.

The narrow road twisted and turned through the valley and in places ran alongside the River Manifold. The rain descended like an unbroken sheet of water and had swollen the river to a dangerous height. Lightning lit up the sky for miles around, and deafening thunder-claps added to the nightmare of the journey. On more than one occasion the men in the coach had to get out and help the coachman, when the carriage wheels stuck in the clinging mud and sweat lathered the terrified horses. Suddenly there was a terrific flash of lightning followed by a deafening crash of thunder, as though an angry God had torn the heavens apart.

This was too much for the horses. Screaming with terror, they fled along the treacherous road, the coachman losing control. Fear drove the horses on but it blinded them to direction, and the close proximity of the river soon brought the terrifying drama to a conclusion. Horses, coach and occupants were flung into the swollen, angry water and, needless to say, they were all drowned.

Today there is a narrow, winding road leading through the valley which was part of the original drive to Throwley Hall. Along this stretch of road the hoof-beats of the phantom horses can still be heard, thundering up to the remains of the Hall. Some years ago a teenaged girl was walking along here towards her home at Ilam, about three miles away. Suddenly she heard the sound of galloping horses coming from behind her. As they grew louder, she distinctly heard the sound of wheels, as though a cart was being pulled at a tremendous speed. The girl moved quickly to one side, stepping off the road as she did so, thinking that whatever was approaching had better be given as much room as possible. The noise came nearer until it was almost deafening. She heard heavy breathing, as if the horses were being driven to their limit. The thundering roar of hooves and the rattle of wheels as they went past her were very real, yet to her horror the girl, now frozen to the spot, saw nothing.

Other people claim to have heard the phantom coach and horses. One man living in Ashbourne claims to have heard them in almost the same place, but in broad daylight – yet again, there was nothing to be seen. Over the last thirty years, scores of people claim to have heard them – even people who knew nothing of the legend – so it would appear that phantom horses still pull the carriage with its ghostly occupants, some 300 years after the tragic event.

10. Spectral Travelling Companions

Britain's railways are over 150 years old. Looking at their run-down condition today, it is difficult for the foreign visitor to imagine that until the amalgamation of the railway companies in 1926 they were the pride of the nation and probably the best in the world. Everyone and everything was carried by rail; the railway revolutionized transport, just as the canals had a century before; it ran like clockwork, and all who worked for the railway companies were jealously proud of their own corner of the vast network. With 150 years of history behind them, the railways of Old England have a number of ghost stories attached to them, particularly some of our older railway stations.

Some years ago, an old porter at Darlington railway station in Durham had a frightening experience when, one cold winter's night, around midnight, he felt chilly and decided to go and get a hot drink and something to eat. There was a porter's cellar where a fire was kept going, and a coalhouse attached to it. He went down the steps, took off his heavy overcoat and had just settled himself on the bench opposite the fire and turned up the gas lamp when a strange man came out of the coalhouse, followed by a big black retriever. As soon as he entered, the porter's eyes were on him and likewise the stranger's eyes were on the porter. They watched each other intently as the stranger moved to the fire and then stood looking at the porter with a curious smile on his face.

All at once he struck out at the frightened porter, who had the impression he had hit him. Quite naturally, he struck back at the figure, but his fist went right through him, striking the stone above the fireplace and scraping the skin from his knuckles. The figure then appeared to stagger back into the fire, uttering a strange and unearthly scream. Immediately the black dog seized the porter by the calf of the leg, causing immense pain. The strange figure recovered, and motioned the dog away. Then dog and figure backed slowly through the closed coalhouse door. The frightened porter lit his lantern and nervously opened the door to the coalhouse and looked around inside, but there was no sight of either man or dog, nor was there any way in which they could have got out, except by the door itself.

Many weeks later the porter discovered that, some years before, a man employed in the booking office had committed suicide by jumping in front of a passing express train. His body had been carried to the cellar prior to its removal by the undertakers. *He* had owned a black retriever, just like the one that had attacked the porter, who later said that no mark or effect remained on the spot where he seemed to have been bitten by the dog.

A similar ghost haunted Middlesbrough railway station in North Yorkshire. At the end of one platform stands what used to be known as 'the dead house', a small stone building often used at the turn of the century as a temporary morgue should any passenger expire on railway property. A young lad by the name of Archer was employed at the station as a telegraphist and to him the 'dead house' seemed eerie and unpleasant. When he was on regular night duty and left his office in the early hours of the morning, he was always uneasy when passing the building alone.

One morning, at about two o'clock, he came out onto the station platform and was walking in the direction of the 'dead house', steeling himself to pass it alone, when to his delight he saw, standing on the platform ahead of him, the familiar figure of Fred Nicholson, one of the signalmen from the box just off the end of the platform. Hoping he would walk with him past the 'dead house', he stepped up to him, but, to his utter amazement and horror, the signalman vanished, as if into thin air!

Feeling very frightened and not knowing what to make of it, Archer went down to the signal box and told the signalman on duty what he had seen. The signalman looked at him in utter amazement and said, 'You have just seen Fred Nicholson? It's impossible. Didn't you know he had been killed by a train this afternoon? His body is lying in the "dead house" at this very moment!'

It was now young Archer's turn to be dismayed; he was perfectly sure in his own mind that he had seen the signalman – and yet the man was dead.

There is a well-authenticated haunting at Dearham Bridge railway station at Maryport in Cumbria, apparently brought about by an incident which took place some time last century. Just after the station – which is on the Barrow-Carlisle line – was opened, a young couple were taking an early evening stroll with their baby, walking towards the railway station, when they stopped on the bridge over the tracks to watch one of the trains which was about to pull out. At the last moment, as the train pulled away from the platform and was about to go under the bridge, the father – for a reason never discovered after all these years – suddenly grabbed the child from its mother's arm and threw it over the bridge in front of the moving train, killing it instantly. The man was subsequently arrested and hanged.

Now local people say that on certain nights of the year, just before a train is due to pass down the line and under the bridge, the screams of the baby can be heard, cutting through the still evening air. Several people who have heard it in recent years have told me they wish they had not been so favoured.

Mayfield railway station in Manchester is now used as a parcels depot, but about twenty-five years ago it was both a terminus and a shunting yard, a dilapidated place of rusty ironwork and crumbling walls, broken roofs and platforms, eerie and cold and believed by many of the station staff to be haunted. There was every reason for the belief, for over the years there have been at least two suicides and several fatal accidents. A man hanged himself in the signal box, a station foreman hanged himself in the gentlemen's lavatory, and a night porter fell fifty feet down a baggage-hoist shaft, killing himself instantly.

Long after the station was closed at night and all was dark, except for the light in the foreman's office, where one man was always on duty, heavy and distinct footsteps were heard approaching from the door of a nearby office; they would pass by the foreman's office and seem to pause at the window, then resume their progress towards the baggage hoist, where they would suddenly cease. Each time anyone went out to see who was there, they never saw anyone but just heard the eerie, echoing footsteps on the deserted platform.

One old porter said at the time that he had been through many nasty experiences in his lifetime but had never come across anything quite as frightening as hearing the phantom footsteps at Mayfield station. He said it was chilling to hear footsteps which you knew did not belong to any earthly body. Apparently he would get a prickly feeling down the spine even before hearing them.

An ex-shunter said that he first heard them at about three o'clock one morning, just as he was about to go off duty. There was no one else in the station at the time, and as he walked towards the office, he heard the footsteps close behind him. A couple of weeks later, he heard them again, but this time he was near the end of the station platform where there was a master switch for all the station lights. He switched on, flooding the whole station with light, but there was no one in sight – yet the footsteps continued towards him. He said they seemed to pass close enough for him to reach out and touch whoever it was, then within a few more seconds they ceased altogether.

Saltney Junction railway station on the A58 road, about a mile from the centre of Chester, was reported to be haunted by a spectral cyclist.

One young man who worked there some years ago had the job of going to the homes of railway guards who were on early shifts and knocking them up. Early one morning he was on his way back to the station after waking a guard when he saw the small dim light of a bicycle approaching. He heard the squeak of the cycle chain as the figure laboured towards him. Yet when it got to within a few feet of him, both figure and squeaking cycle disappeared. The following morning, the young lad made the same journey at the same time – and again the same thing happened. On the third morning he was accompanied by a porter coming on early morning duty, and they both saw the light, then heard the sound of the squeaking bicycle chain, followed by the figure of a man labouring towards them on an old cycle – and again, within a few feet the whole apparition vanished.

It seems that a man who worked on the railway a few years prior to these events, and who rode to work on an old bicycle, had hanged himself at Saltney Junction railway station and since then he has been seen on a great many occasions, always very early in the morning, usually in wintertime, just before the first train of the day is due to pass through.

When the London and North-Western Railway were constructing the line from London to Glasgow, the builders found it would be necessary to bore a tunnel through part of a churchyard, near to where Watford Junction railway station, in Hertfordshire, stands today. Many coffins were exposed and human remains fell onto the railway builders. Once the line was completed, the steam trains roared through Watford rail tunnel unhindered, but the locomotive drivers and their firemen began to realize that the tunnel brought problems of another kind. Every time they fired their boilers, which was necessary at one point in the tunnel, there would be a vicious 'blow-back', and several engine-drivers are known to have been badly burnt by the flames.

An investigation discovered that this occurrence always happened when the engine was directly underneath the graveyard, and the drivers associated this rather dangerous effect with the ghosts of the dead, protesting at the invasion of their privacy.

London has a number of haunted stations, particularly underground stations – Aldgate Station on the Circle line is a typical example, with a variety of sightings – in fact, reports of strange sightings are so regular that they are now entered in the station log.

In the control room, situated in part of the rail tunnel where the older tunnel crossed over the rusty line, footsteps have been heard walking over the sleepers and stopping where the original control room door used to be. A few years ago an engineer looked up and saw the figure of an old lady gently stroking the hair of a colleague who was bending over doing some work on the track. Apparently the man never felt anything, but a few minutes later he made an error which could have been fatal – he touched the conductor rail and 22,000 volts surged through him. Although he was knocked unconscious by the surge of current, he suffered from no after-effects. In more recent years, inexplicable whistling has been heard in this living relic to London's early underground system.

Ickenham station on the A4020 road near Uxbridge is the setting for our final haunted railway station, where at two o'clock on a March morning in the early 1950s a London Transport engineer working in the sub-station at the end of the platform glanced up to see the ghost of a middle-aged woman, wearing a red scarf, standing watching him. Silently she beckoned him to the huge switchboard, where she indicated he should follow her down the adjoining staircase. Not being afraid of the apparition – indeed, she looked solid and life-like – the engineer followed her until she suddenly vanished when nearing the last step. Several other railway workers and early morning passengers have seen this ghost, although no one knows who she is. Local theory is that it is the ghost of a woman who, many years ago, fell from the platform onto the conductor rail and was electrocuted.

We normally associate ghosts with lonely moors, eerie castles and old mansions; one would hardly associate one of the world's busiest international airports with them – yet London's Heathrow Airport is haunted by at least three.

Airline staff, women in particular, have been terrified by an invisible ghost that pants like a dog. They say it creeps up behind them and breathes down their necks, at a spot said to have been haunted by the spirit of the highwayman Dick Turpin, for Heathrow is built on Hounslow Heath, once notorious for highway robbery.

One Pan-American employee reported that she had just left her car in the staff parking lot when the panting began. She said that it sounded like an animal. When she turned round to look, there was nothing there. The panting came closer – right up to her neck in fact, but again when she turned round there was nothing. Two other people, a girl and a man, had moved away having had the very same experience. An airline engineer said that a number of people have heard this weird noise for which there appears to be no logical explanation.

Another ghost which haunts Heathrow is far from invisible. It does not pant or breathe down anyone's neck but it is equally as frightening and is known as 'the ghost in the light grey suit'. One man who saw it in the VIP suite at No. 1 European Terminal was a distinguished diplomat from an African High Commission in London. He fled from one of the airport's VIP lounges, absolutely petrified, and all that could be gleaned from him was that he had seen the bottom half of a man in grey trousers, standing in front of him. The supervisor who told me of this said she believes that she herself has seen the ghost on at least one occasion, but when she looked a second time, the figure had vanished, although there was no way in which anyone could have got out of the lounge without passing by her. An airport policewoman has also experienced what she described as a 'strange presence' in the lounge which she could not explain.

But the strangest of all Heathrow's ghosts is one seen on Runway No. 1. One afternoon in 1970, a police patrol car was cruising round the airport when they received a call over the radio telling them to proceed to Block 6, where a man in a bowler hat had been spotted on the runway. The report came from Airport Ground Operations, who had spotted him on Runway No. 1 – known at Heathrow as 2-8-right. By the time the police car had arrived, the figure had gone, but less than an hour later another radio call sent the car racing back to the same area in search of the man on the runway. Again, when they arrived, there was no one to be found.

By early evening, sightings of the man were becoming more and more frequent. Then a call came from the Airport Control Tower: something was registering on their radar equipment which, judging by its slowness, could only be a human.

Keeping in constant touch by radio, three police cars drove abreast down the runway in a bid to get to the bottom of the mystery. Again they failed.

Later that night, after several more spottings, the three police cars were joined by an airport fire-engine with a searchlight mounted on the roof. Suddenly Aircraft Control picked up a 'blip' on their radar which indicated that the mystery man was back on 2-8-right. They told the police cars to drive in a westerly direction, and when they reached about thirty yards from where the Tower said the figure was recorded on their screen, they switched on the searchlight. They saw nothing.

The message came over, 'You are now ten yards away.'

Still there was no one in sight.

'Five yards away ... four ... three ... two ...'

The voice over the radio yelled, 'Stop! Whatever it is, you have run over it!'

The squad cars jammed on the brakes, and the officers jumped out and began a careful search of the runway, but still they could find nothing.

Through the radio the voice said, 'You must have missed him. He's walking away from you in the other direction. He's behind you!'

Again there was absolutely nothing or no one in sight. Defeated and bewildered, the police crew returned to their base.

Who or what was it? Many staff at Heathrow believe the mystery dates back to 1948, when a DC3 Dakota belonging to Sabena Belgian Airways crashed when attempting to land in thick fog. All twenty-two passengers and the crew were killed. When the airport staff began the gruesome task of probing the wreckage, few of them combing the burnt-out shell of the aircraft were aware of a man wearing a bowler hat and a dark suit until he asked each in turn, 'Excuse me. Have you found my briefcase?' Later, at a crash conference, they all recollected seeing him, but no one knew who he was or how he had drifted out of the fog to the crash site. He was not a survivor of the crash, as checks later revealed that all on board had been killed and all the bodies had been accounted for.

Since that day in 1948 the mysterious 'city gent' has been

spotted a great many times walking along Runway 2-8-right, where the DC3 crashed.

By comparison, it could be said that the ghost which haunts Britain's second largest airport, Manchester International, is quite tame, yet this spectre was seen nearly every day for a period in 1971 and is still to be seen from time to time today. There are somewhere in the region of 4,000 freight-forwarding companies in Britain, all engaged in handling exports and generally trying to improve standards of carrying goods over thousands of air miles. One such firm is C. Claridge & Co Ltd, based at Manchester Airport, whose premises were first reported to be haunted in 1971. These premises were originally the barrack block of 613 Manchester Squadron of the Royal Air Force, and it may be that the ghost is associated with this, although witnesses, mainly cleaners and late-working office staff, describe their spectral workmate as 'an old man'.

There have been various reports of a figure being seen, and other employees reported incidents including strange noises, footsteps, a scream and the unexplained movement of office equipment. On one occasion the police were called when noises were heard coming from the empty building late one night, and a police officer claimed to have seen the apparition, as did a lorry driver. But one of the best recorded sightings was made by one of the company's import clerks, who saw the figure of an old man sitting in a store-room next to his office. When he opened the connecting door, the ghost vanished. Another sighting was made a few days later by one of the night staff who described the old man as having walked through the office in bare feet.

If phantom rail-travellers or fellow airline-passengers seem rather mundane, how would the reader fancy the idea of picking up a phantom hitch-hiker?

The darts match ended early for twenty-six-year-old Roy Fulton. It had not been a lively night, so Roy decided to drive to another pub, the Glider, near his home at Dunstable, Bedfordshire. It was a dark night, and foggy patches hung over the flat, open countryside as he drove towards the village of

Stanbridge. Nearing the houses on the edge of the village, his headlights picked out the dark figure of a youth standing by the roadside, thumbing a lift.

Pulling up just past the young man, Roy waited for him to catch up. He looked at the stranger's face, which was pale and drawn and framed by short, dark, curly hair. He guessed the youth's age to be about twenty. There was nothing unusual about him, except for the shirt he wore, which was an old-fashioned one with a round collar. The young man said nothing as he got into the car. 'I'm going to Dunstable. Where are you for?' Roy asked. The youth pointed towards Totternoe, a village beyond Stanbridge, still saying nothing, so Roy drove on towards Totternoe at a steady 45 mph. The hitch-hiker sat silently.

As the road neared Totternoe, it was lit by street lights. Roy slowed down and, flipping a packet of cigarettes open, he turned to offer one to his passenger – there was no one there! The passenger seat was empty. Roy slammed on the brakes and looked all around him. He stared through the side window, but the road only stretched into empty darkness, and of his fellow traveller there was no sign. A cold draught blew across his neck and a chill gripped his stomach. As his left hand felt the passenger seat, he discovered it was still warm.

As he thought about it, Roy reasoned that the youth could not have got out of the car at the speed of 45 mph, and even if he had, he would have had to open the door, which would automatically have switched on the courtesy light. No light had come on, and the door was firmly shut.

Police at Frome in Somerset report that at least three motorists claim to have been victims of a phantom hitch-hiker. The man, aged between thirty and forty, wearing a check sports jacket, stops cars between the villages of Nunney and Critchill just off the A361 road about four miles south of Frome. He asks to be dropped off at Nunney Catch, but when the cars reach the village, he has disappeared. One driver was so affected by his meeting with the phantom that he had to be admitted to hospital for treatment.

The notorious A38 road, which carves its way across England

from Derby to Cornwall, made even the seasoned driver blanch at its infamous bottlenecks and miles of motionless traffic until much of it was replaced by a motorway. Now the ten-mile stretch of the A38 centred on Wellington in Somerset has an evil reputation far removed from traffic jams: it is haunted by a phantom with a torch in his hand, who tries to flag down passing motorists at night. A report in the *Western Morning News* of August 1970 brought stories of him flooding in.

According to the newspaper, a lady had been travelling from the village of Oake to her home in Taunton late one night when she saw a middle-aged man dressed in a long grey raincoat standing in the middle of the road near the Heatherton Grange Hotel. His face was averted as he appeared to be holding a torch pointing towards the ground. She was confronted by the figure suddenly as she rounded the bend, and as there was no time to brake, she served violently. There was no impact, and a moment later, when she looked, the road was completely empty in both directions.

But it was a long-distance lorry driver, Mr Harold Unsworth of Exeter, who had the worst experience of the mysterious figure. He described how he was driving back to his depot at Cullompton at about three o'clock in the morning when he was flagged down near the Blackbird Inn, about a mile from the Heatherton Grange Hotel, by a middle-aged man in a grey or cream raincoat carrying a torch. The weather was bad, and the man, hatless and with curling grey hair hanging down almost to his collar, seemed so wet and miserable that Mr Unsworth stopped, despite the risk on a lonely road at this early hour, and offered him a lift.

By his speech, the man appeared to be well educated, and he asked to be dropped off about four miles further along the road, at the old bridge at Holcombe. As they travelled, he described with apparent gruesome delight some of the nasty accidents that had happened at the bridge, so Mr Unsworth was not sorry to be rid of his strange passenger. Only a couple of days later, again travelling along the A38 in the early hours, he was astonished to see the same man, standing in the same spot in the same weather conditions. Again he pulled up and the man asked to be dropped off at the bridge at Holcombe.

A month later, in identical conditions, there he was once more: the rain, the darkness, the raincoat and the torch, even the conversation were the same, and Mr Unsworth began to wonder if he was dealing with some kind of lunatic. He was more than relieved when, in the months that followed, although he frequently passed the spot at night, he saw no more of the stranger.

But in November 1968 he was there again and, as in a bizarre film, the sequence of events went round once more – except that on this occasion, when they stopped at the bridge, the man asked if the lorry could wait whilst he collected some cases, as on this occasion he wanted to go further along the road. For over twenty minutes Mr Unsworth waited in the darkness and pouring rain, and then, as the man had not re-appeared, he drove on.

Three miles ahead, however, he saw dimly through the murk of the streaming rain a torch being waved frantically to flag him down. Thinking it was a motorist who had broken down, he slowed down, but when his headlights shone fully on the figure, he saw with rising fear the long, straggling grey hair and grey raincoat of his mysterious passenger. No other vehicle had passed him in either direction at this early hour, and it would have been impossible for anyone to cover the distance on foot in so short a time.

Thoroughly alarmed, Mr Unsworth swerved to one side to pass the gesticulating figure, but as he did so, the man jumped in front of the lorry at such a distance that it was impossible to avoid hitting him. But there was no impact! Mr Unsworth braked hard, nearly jack-knifing his articulated lorry, but fortunately he managed to remain in control and brought it to rest about a dozen yards ahead. He climbed down from his cab and looked back. The figure was still in the road, shaking his fist and swearing loudly at being left behind. Then suddenly he was silent, turned his back – and vanished.

It is impossible to determine the identity of this phantom, as so many motorists and pedestrians have been killed on this stretch of road. Perhaps one day some psychic researcher will discover why this pathetic old man is doomed to seek a lift so desperately from passing vehicles.

11. The Ghosts of London's Theatre Land

The great majority of ghosts do not appear to investigators; they usually appear to the man or woman in the street going about their daily business – people who have scarcely given a ghost a second thought and who, after the sighting and its upsets, plus the attendant scepticism, generally wish they had not been favoured.

Members of the theatrical profession, however, are quite used to seeing mysterious shadows, drifting figures and inexplicable movements when working in some of Britain's older theatres, usually taking them for granted. In fact, if they do a season at a London theatre, most theatricals expect to sight a ghost as a matter of course, for London seems to have more haunted theatres than anywhere else in the country. The reason is obvious, for there are more theatres in the capital than in any other principal British city.

Before the great clown Joe Grimaldi died in 1837, he asked that his head be cut from his body and that he be buried in the shade of St James's Church, Islington, not much more than a hand-clap away from the theatre he loved – the Theatre Royal, Drury Lane.

There has been a Theatre Royal at Drury Lane for more than 300 years; in fact, the present theatre is the fourth built on this site. Grimaldi began his career as a clown here in the 1780s and yet, despite touring the country for the next forty-five years, he continued to return to the Theatre Royal that he loved. This was his theatre, this was where he established himself as the most famous of all English clowns, and this is where he gave his final farewell performance and where, not surprisingly, his ghost can be seen at dead of night, wearing his white clown make-up, staring into the auditorium from one of the boxes. There have also been occasions when his white face has been seen peering out from behind members of the audience in this box.

Dan Leno also scored his biggest success in pantomime at the Theatre Royal. Poor Dan Leno, he went mad and died at the age of forty-three. Some years ago, when playing pantomime at the theatre, the late Stanley Lupino was convinced that he had been confronted by Dan Leno's ghost. He said that after a performance one evening he felt too exhausted to go home and decided to sleep on the couch in his dressing-room. After a while, he distinctly felt that he was not alone, and said later, 'I heard a noise, as if a curtain was being drawn aside. Getting up to investigate, I saw a shadowy figure cross the room and disappear through the door. I was amazed. I went and asked the stage door keeper if he had seen anyone leave – he said he had not!'

Some time later, another actor using the same dressing-room witnessed Dan Leno's ghost. However, this actor was made of less stern stuff than Stanley Lupino – he passed out!

Not many years ago the American actress Betty Jo Jones, a newcomer to the cast of the musical *Oklahoma*, then playing at the Theatre Royal, was having some difficulty in a comedy scene which did not seem to be going over well with the audience. Suddenly she felt 'unseen' hands guide her to a position on the stage from which she began to get her laughs successfully. This happened again on the following night, until she finally got the measure of her audience – and when the scene was going well, she got a kindly pat on the back.

Something of a similar nature happened before the start of the run of another successful musical, *The King and I*, when Doreen Duke was auditioned for a singing role in the show. All the tension and apprehension she felt suddenly left her as the same 'unseen' hands were placed on her shoulders to guide her through the part. As she left the stage, having won the role, she too received a congratulatory pat on the back.

But perhaps the most famous ghost at the Theatre Royal, Drury Lane, is the spectre never seen later than six o'clock in the evening and who is simply known as 'the man in grey'. During the 1850s, when a number of alterations were being made at the theatre, and workmen were busy in the Russell Street side by the upper circle, they were surprised to come across a part of the main wall which rang hollow. They duly reported it and were instructed to break down the wall and see what was behind it. Having broken through, the workmen discovered a small room, in which lay the skeleton of a man with a dagger sticking out from between his ribs.

An inquest was held on the unfortunate victim, at which, in the absence of further evidence, an open verdict was recorded and the skeleton was quietly buried in a little graveyard which, since 1854, has laid under a small space at the corner of Russell Street and Drury Lane, known as Drury Lane Gardens.

Over the years there have been numerous theories put forward to explain the unrecorded crime at the Theatre Royal, the most popular being that the victim was a young Georgian dandy who was stabbed in a quarrel over a beautiful actress, then his body was bricked up in the wall. Whatever the truth of the matter, it seems most likely that it is this murdered man's uneasy but harmless spirit which has haunted the theatre in the years since. He is always given the same description by the many people who have seen him: a man of medium height, dressed in a long grey riding cloak of the eighteenth century, knee breeches and buckled shoes. Beneath the cloak a sword swings as he moves, whilst on his head his powdered wig crowns features which have been described as those of a handsome man with a square jaw. In his hand he often carries a tricorn hat.

This spectre has been seen at least fifty or sixty times over the years, yet strangely he is never seen at night. Theatre cleaners have seen him in the morning and he has appeared at rehearsals and matinées, always moving from one side of the upper circle to the other and vanishing into a wall. Although the identity of the 'man in grey' will probably remain shrouded in mystery, showbiz people are always pleased to see him or hear of his appearance, for it is believed that when he puts in his own personal appearance at Drury Lane it is a good omen for whatever show happens to be running at the time.

*

William Terriss was, at forty-nine, the intrepid hero of popular melodrama at the Adelphi Theatre in the Strand. At seven o'clock on the evening of 16 December 1897 he began a walk which was to lead to his death at the hands of a maniacal bit-player, known amongst other actors at the Adelphi as 'Mad Arthur'.

Terriss lived out of London, so it was his custom each day to dine at the Green Room Club, in Bedford Street, then walk the short distance to the Adelphi, where he would let himself in through a pass-door, to which all the leading players had their own key. On this particular evening Terriss, who was appearing in the play *Secret Service*, was accompanied by an elderly friend, John Greaves. Chatting and laughing, the two men turned into the narrow, gas-lit Maiden Lane, where on arrival at the pass-door Terriss said goodnight to his friend, unbuttoning his frock coat and reaching for his key as he did so. Neither man noticed the silent figure standing in the shadows on the opposite side of the narrow lane – a dark-eyed man with a curled moustache, wearing a long black cape with upturned collar and a slouch hat.

As Terriss put his key in the lock, the man ran from the shadows, crossed the lane and swiftly, silently, plunged a knife into the actor's back. Terriss, taken by surprise, turned to face his assailant and was struck twice more, directly over the heart.

The attacker's real name was Richard Prince. He was aged about thirty-two and had come to London from Scotland to seek fame and fortune on the stage but had failed miserably, being totally unsuitable for the profession. He became the butt of his colleagues' practical jokes and they took to calling him 'Mad Arthur', playing cruelly on his vanity. They teased him that he was destined to become a great actor and that Terriss recognized this, jealously refusing to let him play the heroic roles, which should be his by right. Thus the unstable wretch soon became filled with a burning jealousy.

Following his attack on the great actor, Prince stood by and offered no resistance as he was seized by the police. Terriss in the meantime was carried through the pass-door and twenty minutes later died in the arms of the sobbing Jessie Millward, his leading lady. Prince was subsequently found guilty but insane and was committed to the Broadmoor Criminal Asylum, where he remained until his death in 1947, at the age of seventy-two.

Within weeks of the tragedy, the hauntings of the Adelphi Theatre began. Many actors reported strange tappings coming from William Terriss's old dressing-room, yet at the same time for years no one was prepared to admit the possibility of the noises being made by his spirit – that is, until things finally came to a head in 1928.

Every evening on entering the theatre pass-door in Maiden Lane, Terriss had been in the habit of tapping his walking-stick on the door of his leading lady's room – an affectionate signal to her as he passed on his way to his own dressing-room. The dressing-room was quite large, with three windows and an open fireplace, more like a room in a house than the conventional theatre dressing-room one always imagines.

A well-known comedy actress who was playing at the theatre in 1928 was occupying the dressing-room which had been used by Jessie Millward at the time of the Terriss murder.

It was the actress's practice never to leave the theatre after a matinée; instead a light meal was brought in from a nearby restaurant for her. Following this she would usually stretch out on a comfortable chaise-longue and generally fell asleep until about seven-fifteen, when her dresser would call her and help her prepare for the evening performance. It was during these hours that things began to happen. Often, just as she was about to drop off into a relaxed sleep, the couch would begin to vibrate, then lurch, and often it would seem as though someone was actually lying underneath, kicking it. On another occasion a pale greenish light appeared in front of a dressing-table mirror, which hovered for some time and then disappeared. A knock was often heard at the door, but when the dresser or the actress went to answer it, there was never anyone there.

Over the years there have been frequent reports of footsteps and other strange noises and the feeling of a presence at the Adelphi Theatre, where, although Terriss's old dressing-room no longer exists, the doorway where he was murdered is still to be seen.

Terriss's ghost has never been seen *inside* the theatre, but it was seen in Maiden Lane at some time in the 1950s, when a man (who claimed to know nothing about the story of William Terriss) was walking alone in the lane and saw, coming towards him, a handsome man in rather old-fashioned clothes, who passed by. So striking was he to look at that the man turned to look again, only to find Maiden Lane deserted, although there had not been time for the passer-by to get out of the alley or enter any other building. The meeting had taken place just outside the fatal pass-door.

The management at the Adelphi willingly admit to the fact that night watchmen at the theatre have experienced hearing footsteps and odd noises, and confessed to a feeling of 'being watched'. In 1965 a watchman swore that he could sense something present, very close at hand, as if a person was hiding somewhere nearby, watching him. On other odd occasions the elevators have started working by themselves. They have afterwards been checked and found to be mechanically sound, leaving no explanation whatever for their erratic behaviour.

The Haymarket Theatre – or, to give it its correct title, the Theatre Royal, Haymarket – was built in 1720, at a cost of £1,500, by a carpenter called John Potter and was originally called 'the Little Theatre in the Hay'. John Baldwin Buckstone became manager in about 1853 and until his death lived in a house at the rear of the theatre, which in later years was converted into the theatre's dressing-rooms and offices.

In the years between 1900 and the First World War it was often claimed that a ghost in early Victorian dress, afterwards recognized as Buckstone, had been seen in the dressing-rooms and other parts of the building. It was said that his voice could be clearly heard, quite often, rehearsing the lines of a play in one of the dressing-rooms, and in the years immediately prior to the Great War there were many reports of strange happenings at the theatre. Dressing-room doors flew open, wardrobe doors opened and shut by themselves, and phantom footsteps were often heard in the corridors backstage.

Between the wars, a theatre fireman reported that he had often seen the ghost of Buckstone drifting along the empty theatre passages, and when on one occasion he followed the figure, it vanished after turning a corner. Another time both the fireman and a woman cleaner saw the ghost cross the dress circle on a dark winter's morning. When one cleaner saw the figure of a man standing by a locked door, she said to him, 'You can't go through there, sir. It's all locked up' – at which the figure, just to prove otherwise, turned and walked right through it.

Just before the outbreak of hostilities in 1914, the theatre manager and one of his clerks were half scared to death when, at one o'clock in the morning, they both saw the office door open wide – and then close, of its own accord. This was not caused by a breeze or a faulty lock, and the door was fitted with a heavy spring to keep it shut. There was no one else in the building at the time, and a thorough search failed to reveal anything or anybody who might have opened the door.

In more recent years, Buckstone's ghost was seen by an actor, sitting in an armchair in his dressing-room, and in 1927, when the actress Drusilla Wills was appearing at the Haymarket and was speaking to someone backstage, an elderly man in old-fashioned clothes passed between them. In 1946 the manager, Mr Stuart Watson, had an unnerving experience in the accounts office. In those days it was rather dark and dismal. All of a sudden, every light in the office went out, leaving Mr Watson in complete darkness. As he got up from his desk and crossed the room to check the light switches, he became aware of a terrible feeling of immensely cold air which seemed to surround him and which, for no reason at all, terrified him.

But the most incredible performance of John Buckstone was in 1964, during the run of the show *At the Drop of Another Hat*, when his ghost suddenly appeared on stage, standing behind the wheelchair from which the late Michael Flanders was performing. The stage manager was furious, thinking at first it was a stage-hand and that she would have no other course but to bring down the curtain. Then the figure moved and she saw, to her utter amazement, that this was no ordinary stage-hand but a man in a long black frock coat who, just as suddenly as he appeared, vanished again.

The last memory of the London of 1918 that a young British Army officer took back with him to the nightmare of the Western Front was of the high-kicking ladies of the chorus of the Coliseum Theatre, St Martin's Lane.

Like a good many young men, he had spent the last few precious hours of his leave laughing and cheering in this lavishly decorated theatre until, the dream over and reality beckoning, he left the warmth of the dress circle, exchanging it for the cold night air of the Strand, which he crossed to Charing Cross railway station, where he boarded a troop train to oblivion. On 3 October 1918 he was killed going 'over the top' in one of the last major offensives of the war.

On the very night he died, his ghost was seen at the Coliseum. His khaki uniformed figure was recognized as it moved down the stairs of the dress circle, turning in, two or three rows from the front, just as the lights dimmed for the show to commence. Between the wars the khaki-clad ghost was seen on numerous occasions by various people in the old theatre, but it seems that since the Second World War it has been reported less frequently.

The St James's Theatre used to stand in King Street. It was opened in December 1835 and closed after the final performance of *Its the Geography that Counts* on Saturday 27 July 1957. For a good number of years the theatre was said to be haunted by the ghost of a courier who used to come from Marlborough House, just at the back of King Street, on the orders of King Edward VII, to escort Lillie Langtry by an underground tunnel under Angel Court, where the stage door was, direct to the King's presence.

When the actress Joan Harben was playing in *Pride and Prejudice* at the St James's, she was alone in her dressing-room, putting on her dressing-gown, when she felt herself being helped firmly into it. So certain was she that someone was helping her that she nearly fainted when, turning round to thank them, she found that there was no one with her.

Once it was decided the theatre was to close down, the ghost began to be seen with amazing regularity, particularly by the theatre firemen. But it was on the night of the theatre's closure that he was witnessed most plainly and was to make his final appearance. By tradition, on the last night of a show, the star usually gives a small party for the cast. Because 27 July was also the last night of the theatre's life, a second party was held. The late John Gregson, the star of the play, gave his party in his dressing-room, and Vivien Leigh, joint owner of the theatre, gave a party on the stage – one can well imagine the emotional atmosphere on such an occasion.

A young stage-hand who was hired only for this final production felt depressed at the demise of this fine old theatre. He wandered from backstage through the pass-door and into the auditorium. The audience had long since gone, the auditorium was almost in darkness, and there should have been no one there but the stage staff and the fireman, who was locking up at the front of the house. But in the dress circle there was a man staring into the auditorium. It was difficult to make out his features in such a bad light, or how he was dressed, but there was no doubting that he was there.

The astonished stage-hand called out, 'Hello. Who's there?' The man did not move, but a soft voice in his ear startled him, 'He's often there. He's the theatre ghost.' Hair starting to bristle, the stage-hand spun round to find himself looking into the friendly face of the theatre fireman, who had walked quietly up to him. 'He's been there quite a lot since we knew the theatre was to be pulled down.'

The young man had never heard of the theatre ghost, and the fireman went on to explain that no one knew who he really was, as no one seemed able to get close enough to identify him. He said that some people thought he was the ghost of an actor who had been wrongfully dismissed, whilst others said he was someone of importance connected with Marlborough House.

The two men looked up to the dress circle again, but the man had gone. He too had given his final performance.

With the exception of Nellie, all the girls who work at the Gargoyle Club in Soho are strippers. The club is said to be the oldest nightclub in Europe, and Nellie is said to be the ghost of Nell Gwynne, who worked as a barmaid at the Cock & Magpie, a beerhouse on Drury Lane, before her association with King Charles II. She was a friend of many actors and lived in Soho, in a house in Dean Street, next to the old Royalty Theatre.

The ghost of Nellie is often glimpsed in the early hours and is said to be 'grey and shadowy', wearing a high-waisted period dress and a large flowered hat. She has about her an overpowering perfume which lingers, making the room smell of gardenias. Apparently she is seen to glide across the floor and disappear into a liftshaft.

One man who saw her a few years ago said that he witnessed the ghost of an elderly woman whom he did not recognize as looking remotely like Nell Gwynne, who died at the age of thirty-seven and not in old age. He said he thought she was more likely to be the ghost of Fanny Kelly, who built the old Royalty Theatre next door which was destroyed by German bombs during the Second World War.

The Royalty Theatre opened under the management of Fanny Kelly in 1840. Fanny was an actress herself, well known in Drury Lane, and she lived at 73 Dean Street. The theatre was built at the rear of her house by her patron, the Duke of Devonshire. It soon became known as Miss Kelly's Theatre and Dramatic School, and one of those known to have worked there was Charles Dickens, who played Bobadil in Ben Jonson's *Every Man in His Humour* in September 1845.

Unfortunately Fanny's venture as a theatrical entrepreneur was hardly a success, and the theatre closed down for lack of financial support, undergoing several changes over the next few years. It became known for a short time as the Soho Theatre, and then, in 1905, it re-opened as the New Royalty Theatre. It was at that period that the ghost of Fanny Kelly became a regular feature. Many people saw the apparition of a woman dressed in grey, sitting quietly in a stage box. A number of staff claimed to have seen the ghost, which in general appeared in the stage box at about one o'clock in the morning, particularly if a dress rehearsal was in progress.

Fanny's ghost was also seen walking down the staircase of what was once her house and later became an integral part of the theatre. It crossed to the centre of the vestibule and inexplicably vanished.

Many people seem to think that when Fanny's business venture collapsed she committed suicide and her spirit, jealous of the success of others in later years, wandered the theatre. With the destruction of her theatre and the subsequent building of an office block over the site, Miss Kelly's restless spirit ought to have found eternal peace but it seems she just moved next door to cause a bit of a nuisance at the Gargoyle

Club – and trying to put the blame on Nell Gwynne.

Like Fanny Kelly's Royalty Theatre, there is now nothing left of the old Collins' Music Hall, perhaps the most famous of all London's music halls – nothing, that is, except its ghost, which survived the disastrous fire that caused the old theatre to go out of business.

Collins' Music Hall was started by an Irishman called Vagg, who toured the music halls of the country under the stage name of Sam Collins, 'The Singing Chimney Sweep'. For years his ghost had haunted the place, in particular his old office, which overlooked Islington Green. The ghost was normally active round about the time of the first interval, when doors would slam shut of their own accord, even after they had been wedged open.

It is said that someone who once accepted the offer of a night on the couch in Sam Collins' old office abandoned the idea soon after settling down, when he swore he felt the touch of ice-cold fingers on his throat and face. Dan Leno's ghost got about too, for he is also thought to have haunted Collins' Music Hall. He would turn up at rehearsals, always sitting in the same seat and snapping his fingers impatiently, if he disapproved of a performance – something he always did in his own lifetime.

In 1972 reports reached the Press which brought to light an unusual haunting at a bingo hall, a converted theatre in Clapham High Street, a couple of miles from the centre of London. Not only has the ghost been sensed, it has been sighted and also recorded on tape. Several people have researched this weird phenomena, and their descriptions appear to tally each time the ghost has been observed.

It appears that around the turn of the century a music hall artist, who usually appeared at the bottom of the bill but had ambitions to become another Dame Nellie Melba, realized – or more probably was bluntly informed – that she had neither the qualities nor the tenacity and strength of purpose needed to achieve her ambition. One night she clambered onto the roof of the building, alone and despairing, and there she sang to the starry skies. On completion of her operatic aria, she threw herself from the roof to her death – or so the story goes. Much more likely is the theory that she was a drunken young woman who, in her cups, decided to let the world hear her sing and who, whilst staggering across the roof, missing her footing in the dark and plunged through a skylight to her death. Whichever way it was, her spirit has since returned to haunt the rooftop and the stairway leading to it.

In 1972 doors which had previously been bolted were found to have been opened, and the security men heard loud bangs and footsteps going up the stairs and out onto the roof. Puzzled by these incidents, one of the security men left a tape recorder running on the stage all night, and when it was played back the following day, the sound of a door banging was heard and, most amazing of all, a woman's voice singing snatches of opera.

In 1973 the hauntings had become alarmingly regular, and some members of the staff claimed to have seen a vague figure resembling a headless woman standing in the stage area. Unfortunately, nothing more can be discovered about this most fascinating ghost, as, because of the trouble the publicity caused in 1973, the management steadfastly refuse to discuss it.

When Joan Littlewood first established her Theatre Workshop at the old Theatre Royal, Bow, some of the players who had difficulty in finding lodgings lived for a time in the dressing-rooms. One such person was old George, the self-appointed and unpaid caretaker who, although he had a home of his own nearby, preferred to sleep in the boiler room and live off the tips which people gave him for doing odd jobs and running errands.

There are many people who still remember old George with affection. For twenty years he had lived at the theatre, saving all the odd sixpences and shillings he had earned as tips until, when he died in 1968, he left behind an old tin box full of money. He is reputed to have left it hidden in a safe place, guarded by the ghost of the theatre. On his deathbed, old George said he had left the ghost to keep the hiding-place a secret and told everybody who crowded round his bed to catch his last words, 'The money is in a tin box with a book saying who it should be given to.'

Who is the ghost who guards George's fortune? Does the

money still remain undiscovered somewhere on the theatre site?

Although I am unable to answer the latter question, the ghostly figure, which has been seen several times, has been described as that of a small, tubby person, dressed in brown. People have often been aware of his presence, particularly late at night, although they admit that they felt the spirit was friendly towards them and that there was no need to be afraid. He is thought to be the ghost of Frederick Fredericks, the man who built the theatre in 1880 and under whose management, in the early days, it was extremely successful.

It is suggested that the ghost appears once a night, just to make sure that his initials, 'F.F.', remained in the centre of the proscenium arch, for on the day they are painted out or removed, the Theatre Royal would fall down.

This last story was brought to my notice whilst I was researching this book. I am most grateful to Mr Tony Ortzen for allowing me to quote the article from the *Psychic News* of November 1983.

In what could prove to be a classic case of spirit communication and evidence of survival after death, medium Leslie Flint told the newspaper how a long-dead usherette, seen by himself and his companion in a packed theatre, subsequently returned at a later séance. The unusual story began in March 1972, when Leslie and his companion Bram Rogers bought tickets for the Lyric Theatre in Shaftesbury Avenue.

Leslie stopped to ask an elderly usherette how much the programmes cost. She told him and he tendered the correct money, which she slipped into the bead-embroidered dolly-bag on her wrist. Leslie took the programme to his seat and, glancing through it, remarked to his companion, 'Did you see that usherette? Wasn't she old-fashioned?' The men had both noticed how out of place the woman had appeared, quite unlike the other female staff at the theatre. She was thin, of average height, and wore a long black bombazine skirt with a black taffeta blouse. Round her neck was a velvet ribbon with a cameo brooch pinned on it, and her hair was scraped back into a bun.

At the interval the pair, still intrigued by her appearance, decided to make enquiries about the usherette. Leslie asked in one bar, whilst Bram asked in the other, but the staff claimed no knowledge of such a woman. Fascinating stuff, but the best is yet to come.

Some months later Leslie and Bram were at a séance when through the medium came the Cockney voice of a woman who said her name was Miss Nellie Klute. The voice was that of a sprightly elderly woman and could be described as chirpy and forthright. She said she used to sell programmes in various London theatres – in particular, the Lyric and the Globe. Nellie said she had loved the theatre and did not have far to travel to work, as she had lived in Drury Lane, 'in the buildings'. She was there at the turn of the century until her death in a Zeppelin raid during World War I.

It transpired that Nellie was born and bred in London, of Jewish extraction, and she could trace her family back to the days of Nell Gwynne. Both her parents were interested in the theatre, and her mother used to sew 'spangles and things' for some of the clowns, including the famous Grimaldi.

Asked about the old-time theatre, Nellie began to reminisce. She said she could remember all the lovely old plays: Forbes Robertson in *The Passing of the Third Floor Back*, Oscar Asche and Lily Braystone in *Chu Chin Chow*, which she said was a real spectacle in which they filled the whole theatre with incense. 'In those days they were great actor-managers,' she said, 'who spent their entire fortune on one production in a great gamble. You can't see 'em doing that now, they ain't dedicated. In the old days they would invest every half-penny, begging, borrowing, stealing. But what shows! What productions!'

Nellie then went on to describe the old gas lighting, which she said was soft and pleasant. Electricity was too harsh by comparison with the old gas light. She recalled seeing all the great performers of her day, such as Irving, Terry and William Terriss, and remembered seeing Marie Tempest, 'when she was a slip of a girl', in musical plays. Of Marie Tempest she said, 'She had a nice little voice, did Marie. Another I saw was Lily Elsie. She was a nice, dainty, sweet little thing. She hadn't got a good voice, but she was lovely.'

She recalled seeing Sir Henry Iriving in *The Bells*, at the old

Lyceum. 'Wonderful scene they had when he heard the bells,' she said. 'They had this kind of transformation scene at the back. The inn disappeared and all of a sudden you saw all the snow, the old Jew on his sleigh. It was marvellous.' She talked about Beerbohm Tree, saying that he spent thousands of pounds on his productions and that she remembered seeing him in a production of *King John*. 'We had a marvellous orchestra in them days too,' she recalled, 'none of this tinny stuff.'

Nellie told how theatre-goers used to ride in carriages, all lined up in the side streets. The women looking elegant, the men all dressed up, in the circle. 'You wouldn't dare go up into the circle unless you was all dressed up,' she said. The dead usherette remembered the Gaiety Theatre and George Edwardes and recalled some of the musical shows she saw there – *The Merry Widow, Lilac Domino, Véronique* and the lovely *Swing Song*. She commiserated with today's performers, adding, 'There are some very good actors, but it's the rubbish they have to be in. It's a shame.'

One member of the group at the séance mentioned the show *Maid of the Mountains* and Nellie was quick to respond, 'Oh, that was Josie Collins. She was a bit fat, but she had a marvellous voice. She looked very Jewish, of course, but she was striking in a way. There was no doubt about it, she had the best voice on the stage at the time, in that sort of thing.' She went on to say, 'The theatre was a wonderful place at the turn of the century. You got the real feeling about it. The gold, the plush, the smell of oranges in the gallery ... After the curtain had gone up, I saw the same show, night after night, I was never on stage, but I never missed a performance and I loved every minute of it.' She recalled how sometimes she would think, 'Oh, she was good tonight,' or 'She's had one over the eight tonight.' She said, 'They used to have their stout round the back. The man at the door, old Will, used to get them rounds of stout and they would have a proper old beano.'

When one of the group asked if the gas light of the old time theatres was dangerous, Nellie brushed the question aside. 'Oh, they used to have wire netting over it,' she said, 'but there was one or two nasty things when someone's dress caught light, but it wasn't all that dangerous. It had a wonderful quality, you know.' She remembered when the Lyceum converted to electricity and related how Sir Henry Irving had taken it out, because he thought it was terrible the way it spoilt the scenery. Referring to theatre ghosts, she said she thought most theatres were haunted, because people had loved them so much and there was such a wonderful atmosphere.

Nellie then proved she had not lost her sense of fun, by sending the group into roars of laughter with reminiscences of the occasional mishaps she had seen on stage – such as the actor who disappeared via a trap-door before his cue, leaving the leading lady stranded on stage!

Following the séance, two theatrical members of the group checked all the details Nellie had given them and found they were all correct, and confirmation that Nellie Klute had existed came a few months later, when a copy of the tape-recording made at the séance was sent to Mrs Pauline Leiberman, who had known about Nellie all her life and was able to fill in the blank details.

It appears that during the Spanish Inquisition many Jewish people left Spain. Mrs Leiberman's forebears had come over to England, but Nellie's emigrated first to Holland, where they took the name of Klute. One of Nellie's ancestors had been a rabbi in London's East End.

The only question which now remains is why Nellie Klute was suddenly visible to the two men some sixty years after her death. Was it because of the intensity of her love of the theatre, that she had been able, in some way, to transfigure the real usherette?

The End?

Well not quite ... for the ghosts of England's past will always
   be with us.
Tomorrow – today will become yesterday.
And today is the birthday of tomorrow's ghosts.
(If you see what I mean.)

                                        Terence Whitaker

Index

St Magnus the Martyr, 128
Salisbury, Countess of, 14
Saltney Junction railway station, 188
Samlesbury, Gospatrick de, 38
Samlesbury Hall, 38
Sandford Orcas Manor, 72
Savoy Bingo Hall, Folkestone, 91
Scarborough Caastle, 23
Scott, Sir Walter, 57
Secret Service, 200
Seymour, Lord Edward, 24
Seymour, Jane, 24, 28
Shakespeare, William, 41
Siddons, Sarah, 83, 93, 95
Simpkins Brothers, 93
Singleton, Adam de, 119
Sitwell, Edith, 52
Sitwell, Sir George, 52
Sitwell, Osbert, 52
Sitwell, Sacheverell, 52
Smalman, Major, 177
Speke Hall, 39
Sondes, Sir George, 73
Sondes, Reginald, 73
Southey, Robert, 57
Southworth, Lady Dorothy, 38
Southworth, Sir John, 38
Stephen, King, 141
Sussex, Earl of, 118

Tempest, Marie, 210
Tempest, Richard, 43
Terriss, William, 200, 210
Testwood House, 70
Thames Television, 82
Theatres
  Adelphi, London, 200
  City Varieties, Leeds, 81
  Coliseum, London, 204
  Collins Music Hall, London, 207
  Empire, Sunderland, 80
  Gaiety, London, 211
  Globe, London, 210
  Grand, Lancaster, 83
  Haymarket, London, 202
  Lyceum, London, 211
  Lyric, London, 209

New Tyne, Newcastle, 79
Old Vic, Bristol, 95
Royalty, London, 205
St James, London, 204
Star Music Hall, Bolton, 81
Theatre Royal, Bath, 88
Theatre Royal, Bow, 208
Theatre Royal, Bristol, 94
Theatre Royal, Drury Lane, 197
Theatre Royal, Margate, 86
Theatre Royal, Northampton, 84
Theatre Royal, Winchester, 92
Theatre Royal, York, 141
Thorne, Sarah, 87
Throwley Hall, 183
Timberbottom Skulls, 112
Top Rank Bingo Hall, Sutton, 90
Tower of London, 13
Townshend, Dorothy, 49
Townshend, Marquis of, 49
Trigg, Henry, 78
Tunstead Farm, 105
Turpin, Dick, 167, 173, 190
Turton Tower, 111

University College, 66
Unknown Warrior, 136
Unsworth, Harold, 195

Verney, Ruth, 68
Verney, Sir Edmund, 67
Victoria, Queen, 22
Villiers, George, 155
Villiers, Lord Francis, 30

Waldegrave family, 143
Wall, St John, 120
Wallace, Katherine, 47
Walpole, Sir Robert, 49
Warbleton Priory Farm, 107
Warboys, Sir Robert, 64
Wardley Hall, 109
Warrene, Lady Blanche de, 26
Warwick, Earl of, 23
Watford Junction railway station, 189
Watson, Stuart, 203
Watton Abbey, 139